way, and mer-ri-ly
he Sad tyres in a Mile-a : Your paltry
ſtare for, when little or nothing ſoon
Caſt care away, care away, let ſorrow
ſing, laugh and ſing, or if you pleaſe,

Shakespeare's Use of Music

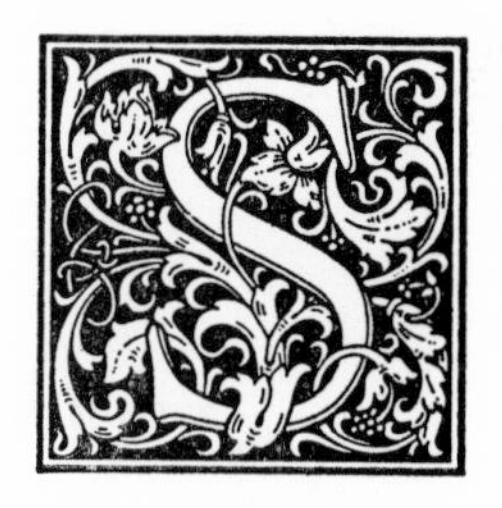

HAKESPEARE'S USE OF MUSIC:

THE FINAL COMEDIES

by

JOHN H. LONG

UNIVERSITY OF FLORIDA PRESS

GAINESVILLE · 1961

To J.W.L. and B.H.E.

A UNIVERSITY OF FLORIDA PRESS BOOK

PUBLISHED WITH ASSISTANCE FROM
THE FORD FOUNDATION

L. C. CATALOGUE CARD NO. 61-17588

PRINTED BY CONVENTION PRESS, JACKSONVILLE, FLORIDA

SHAKESPEARE'S USE OF MUSIC: A TRILOGY

☆ A STUDY OF THE MUSIC AND ITS PERFORMANCE IN THE ORIGINAL PRODUCTION OF SEVEN COMEDIES

☆☆ THE FINAL COMEDIES

☆☆☆ THE TRAGEDIES (IN PREPARATION)

Acknowledgments

T IS WITH PLEASURE AND GRATITUDE THAT I acknowledge here the generosity of the following publishing companies in permitting me to quote from their books: J. M. Dent & Sons, Ltd.; E. P. Dutton & Co., Inc.; Ginn and Co.; George G. Harrap & Co., Ltd.; Kamin Publishers; Methuen & Co., Ltd.; Oxford University Press, Inc.; Routledge & Kegan Paul, Ltd.; Yale University Press.

Contents

Musical Illustrations

Introduction

N THIS BOOK I OFFER THE RESULTS OF A STUDY of Shakespeare's use of music in the final comedies —*The Taming of the Shrew, The Merry Wives of Windsor, Measure for Measure, All's Well That Ends Well, Pericles, Cymbeline, The Winter's Tale,* and *The Tempest*—as they were probably produced between the years 1600-1614. This study is a continuation of an earlier one begun in a preceding book, *Shakespeare's Use of Music.* As in the first volume, here I attempt to determine the functions of the performed music in the comedies, the manner of performance, the original musical scores used (when possible), and the significance of these data to peripheral problems of interpretation, text, staging, stage history—in sum, Shakespeare's development as an artist.

In presenting my material, I have tried to meet the interests of a rather broad audience including students of Elizabethan music, drama in performance, and literature, as well as the producer of Shakespeare faced with practical problems. I cannot, therefore, claim to satisfy completely the scholar in any one of these exacting disciplines. Even if I possessed the necessary scholarship—to which I make slight claim—I would defeat the purpose of this book if I addressed it to students in a specialized field. Rather, I hope it may evoke in the reader that sense of kinship and close companionship between the arts which, accompanied by an alert eye for the practical, was one of the remarkable characteristics of the English Renaissance.

Even so, I have tried to treat the subject with as much accuracy as my knowledge of it permits. For my texts I have used both modern editions and the Quartos and First Folio. All quotations (excepting those from *Pericles*) are from the Folio edition unless otherwise noted. Line numbers follow the Globe edition. The only tampering I have done is to modernize the early "u"-for-"v" convention. Where I found it necessary to treat musical technicalities, in each case I consulted competent musicologists. In the presentation of facts and authoritative opinion, I have used frequent documentation. I therefore trust that my conclusions are valid and hence of some value to the serious students of literature and music.

In selecting the musical examples, I chose either scores written for Shakespeare's text by composers contemporary with him, or music written or published before 1650 which is representative of the Jacobean period during which Shakespeare's later comedies were staged. Those scores associated closely with Shakespeare have been photographically reproduced and, where necessary for clarity, transcribed into modern notation. I regret that I could not supply complete instrumental or vocal parts for the benefit of the producer: in some cases all the parts have not been found; in others the cost is prohibitive.

While the Bibliography includes some basic titles listed in the first volume, it is largely a supplement and should not be considered as a full survey of source material.

For a discussion of the musical instruments, musical forms, notation, and songs of Shakespeare's time, I suggest that the reader turn to the first two chapters of the preceding volume.

My discussion of the Neo-Platonic music in *The Tempest* (Chapter VII) covers some of the same material, and arrives at somewhat the same conclusion, as does a study by John P. Cutts ("Music and the Supernatural in 'The Tempest': a Study in Interpretation," *Music & Letters,* XXXIX, 1958). Since my manuscript was independently written and originally placed in the hands of the University of Florida Press in 1957, and since there are no serious contradictions in the two studies, I have made no changes in my manuscript. It is only natural that two students working in the same area with similar materials should sometimes arrive at similar conclusions.

The most pleasant part of writing this introduction is the acknowledgment of the cheerful and able assistance given me by individuals and institutions. Each debt of gratitude recalls some act of sympathy and generosity from each of the following, and from many others not named here: T. Walter Herbert, University of

Florida; Lewis F. Haines, Director of the University of Florida Press; Charles Haywood, Queens College; Peter Seng, Northwestern University; Jerome Rosen, Director of the Ancient Instruments Ensemble of St. Louis; and the Directors and Staffs of the following institutions: The Folger Shakespeare Library; The Music Division of the New York Public Library; The Music Division of the Library of Congress; The Henry E. Huntington Library; The Library of the Royal College of Music; The British Museum; and the Bodleian Library. I am also grateful for the money grants given me by the Trustees of the Folger Shakespeare Library in the summer of 1951, and the Trustees of the John Simon Guggenheim Foundation in 1957, which latter grant aided me in the final revision of the manuscript here published.

For special technical assistance I wish to thank Dorothy E. Mason, Reference Librarian of the Folger Shakespeare Library, both for her aid in tracing documents and for helping me from her own formidable knowledge of early English music; Joel Newman, Department of Music, Columbia University, for his aid in transcribing the lute tablature of the manuscript song, "Get you hence"; and Betty Marzan, Morehead, Kentucky, for her days of tedious and exacting work in preparing the music notation for publication.

Any errors which, in spite of such able assistance, appear in this book can be attributed only to the author.

JOHN H. LONG

Greensboro, North Carolina
June 26, 1961

ONE

The Taming of the Shrew and *The Merry Wives of Windsor*

THE TWO FARCES WITH WHICH WE BEGIN THIS examination of Shakespeare's use of music are not generally considered among his masterpieces; moreover, they contain comparatively little music. For these two reasons *The Taming of the Shrew* and *The Merry Wives of Windsor* have been placed arbitrarily in a single chapter. The difficulty of assigning a close date of composition to *The Shrew* also provides a convenient excuse for discussing both plays at one time. The date usually assigned to *The Merry Wives,* 1600, falls about the middle of the extremes, 1593-1607, suggested as dates for *The Shrew.*

Actually there is little new in Shakespeare's employment of music in *The Shrew.* At first glance it would appear that he spent little time or thought on the music. A winding of hunting horns for the entrance of the Lord from his sport (Induction, I, i) seems a rather feeble gesture when we compare these horns with those which sound so ingeniously in the hunting scene of *A Midsummer Night's Dream.*[1] Another gesture—the trumpets which peal at the entrance of the Lord's players (I, i)—recalls "Tawyer with a trumpet" who precedes the clowns entering to present their most brief and tedious tragedy of Pyramus and Thisbe.

Even so, the few musical episodes within the play contribute much to the spirit of the farce. Consider the drunken Sly as he reclines in the Lord's palace, soon to be awakened amid sybaritic luxury. The Lord adds a final touch to his jest (I, i, 50, 51): "Procure me Musicke readie when he wakes,/ To make a dulcet and a heavenly sound."[2] The musicians are brought in. When he awakes, Sly is cajoled by the Lord, who asks (I, ii, 37, 38): "Wilt thou have

Musicke? Harke Apollo plaies,/ And twentie caged Nightingales do sing. *Musick.*" The ears of the confused Sly are then titillated by a consort of musicians playing, probably, a delicate aubade, or "hunts-up," accompanied by a twittering of artificial birdcalls.[3]

Do we not recall the lark which sings such sweet divisions at Juliet's balcony? And we find ourselves recollecting a similar scene in *A Midsummer Night's Dream* as the dainty Titania plies Bottom with her offer of music: "What, wilt thou heare some musicke, my sweet love." The comic device—the exaggerated disparity between the fairy music offered by Titania and Bottom and the song of the nightingales and Sly—could only be ludicrous, especially as the contrast is augmented, in the Lord's jest, by the dulcet and heavenly music of the consort.

The music of the consort was doubtless performed by some of the implied swarm of servants hovering about Sly's bed. A combination of lute, mandore, and recorder would provide music suitably light and airy for the scene. An appropriate score might be the music Robert Jones composed for Anthony Munday's lyric, "Beauty sat Bathing," which, performed before Sly, should add to the comedy of the scene. Figure 1 presents the lyric from Munday's *A Banquet of Dainty Conceits* (1588) as set to music by Jones in his *Ultimum*

FIGURE 1.—Beauty sat Bathing

Vale, or the Third Book of Ayres of 1, 2 and 4 Voyces (1608) and transcribed by John Gibbon, *Melody and the Lyric*, p. 57.

The offstage marriage of Petruchio and Katherine is described by the amazed Gremio. At the conclusion of his account, the approach of the festive wedding party is signaled by the music of minstrels, as Gremio states: " . . . after me the rout is comming, such a mad marryage never was before: harke, harke, I hear the minstrels play. *Musicke playes. Enter Petruchio, Kate, Bianca, Hortensio, Baptista.*"

The madcap quality of Kate's marriage supplies the dramatic focus of the scene. The minstrels mentioned by Gremio should be considered as a part of the setting. These strolling fiddlers, who were not above using such occasions to pick a few pockets on the side, are more suitable for Petruchio's purpose than the more sedate municipal waits who were frequently hired to play for weddings. The band of minstrels probably consisted of two or three fiddlers and a cittern player and a taborer. Fiddlers usually played for weddings and the dancing thereafter.[4] A tune jaunty enough to fit the occasion is Antony Holborne's "The Night Watch," one of the pieces in his *Pavans, galliards, almains, and other short aeirs* (1599). The copy

FIGURE 2.—The Night Watch

in the Huntington Library, from which Figure 2 was transcribed, contains only the cantus and bassus parts as shown.

The remaining music in the play consists of two ballad fragments sung, or more likely bellowed, by Petruchio as he orders his servants about in his country home (IV, i, 143, 148, 149): "Where is the life that late I led" and "It was the Friar of Ordersgray,/As he forth walked on his way." These ebullient outbursts defy efforts to identify their tunes. They seem to be snatches of ballads for which several tunes might have been used. The first ballad fragment was apparently fixed in Shakespeare's mind, for he uses it, as the New Cambridge editors and others note, in 2 *Henry IV,* V, iii.

For practical purposes the fragments are here set to portions of the old ballad "Lusty Gallant," as found in Gibbon, *Melody and the Lyric,* p. 65, and a "Coranto" (No. 22) from Thomas Morley's *First Booke of Consort Lessons* (1599 and 1611), respectively.

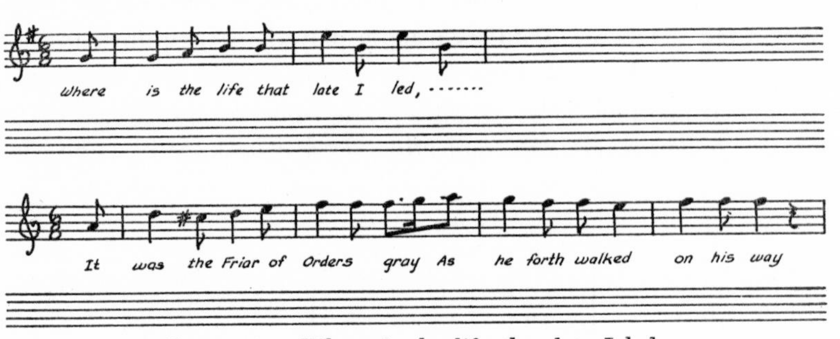
Where is the life that late I led, ...
It was the Friar of Orders gray As he forth walked on his way

FIGURE 3.—Where is the life that late I led
It was the Friar of Ordersgray

To sum up, there is a half-hearted, casual quality about Shakespeare's treatment of the music in *The Shrew* which suggests a degree of haste or lack of interest strange to the practices we have observed in previous comedies. Perhaps he found music uncongenial to the farce type, a point made earlier in connection with *The Comedy of Errors;* perhaps he included music because its use was customary, or, no slight reason, to provide some work for the playhouse musicians. The birdcalls, if actually used, supply the only spark of novelty.

* * * * * * * * * * *

According to the legend generally accepted, at least in part, by students of Shakespeare, *The Merry Wives of Windsor* was written at the request of Queen Elizabeth who wished to see a play of "Falstaff in love." At any rate, sometime during 1600 and 1601 Shakespeare wrote the slight, gay, and rowdy farce in which Falstaff, in one sense, is shown "in love." In 1602 the play was published in quarto purporting to be "as it hath bene divers times Acted by the right Honorable my Lord Chamberlaines servants. Both before her Maistie, and else-where."

The text of the play has been studied by several acute scholars and has been presented in modern editions conforming closely to the version printed in the First Folio of 1623. The Folio version we may therefore accept for our purpose as the basic text of the play, with one notable exception—the miniature masque in V, v. For this scene we shall use the text of the 1602 Quarto.[5]

Mistress Quickly furnishes the play with its initial music, such as it is, in I, iv. That busybody is surprised in her conference with Peter Simple by her master, Dr. Caius. After hiding Peter in a closet, she feigns composure by singing the refrain of a bawdy ballad as Caius enters the room (lines 38-44):

> *Ru.* Out alas: Here comes my Master.
> *Qu.* We shall all be shent: Run in here, good young
> man: goe into this Closset: he will not stay long:
> what John Rugby? John: what John I say? goe John, goe
> enquire for my Master, I doubt he be not well, that hee
> comes not home: (*and downe, downe, adowne a. etc.*)
> *Ca* Vat is you sing? I doe not like des-toyes. . . .[6]

The fragment sung by Mistress Quickly could have been a part of several songs of the period since the burden, "downe, downe, adowne," was a common one. The editor of the Arden edition of the play suggests the ballad of "Donkin Dargeson" as a likely choice, noting that one verse of the song appears in *The Isle of Guls* (1606). This verse is the following:

> But lante tanta the girles are ours,
> We have won 'em away to dargison,
> An ambling nag and doun, a doun,
> We have borne her away to dargison. . . .[7]

The tune of "Donkin Dargeson" is shown in Figure 4 as it appears in William Chappell's *Popular Music of the Olden Time,* I, 65, under the caption "Dargason or A mery Ballet of the Hathorne Tree to be sung to the tune of Donkin Dargeson." As apparent, we find in this tune the ancestor of the well-known jig lately called "The Irish Washerwoman."

But lantatant the girls are ours We've won 'em away to dargison An ambling nag and
doun, a doun We've borne her away to dargi - son ......
Her cherry red lip a doun, a doun.

FIGURE 4.—Donkin Dargeson

Another example of a song rendered in a fragmentary manner to indicate inner discomposure occurs when Sir Hugh quavers out a few lines from Marlowe's lyric, "Come live with me, and be my love," with an interpolated line from the 137th Psalm. The good parson, fearfully awaiting his duelling opponent, Dr. Caius, sings in a vain attempt to keep up his courage. In his confusion, instead of singing a pious psalm he sings lines from the amorous lyric. We find him waiting for Caius (III, i, 11-30):

> *Evan.* 'Please my soule: how full of Chollors I am, and trempling of minde: I shall be glad if he have deceived me: how melancholies I am? I will knog his Urinalls about his knaves costard, when I have good opportunities for the orke: 'Please my soule: *To shallow Rivers to whose falls: melodious Birds sings Madrigalls: There will we make our Peds of Roses. and a thousand fragrant posies. To shallow;* Mercie on mee, I have a great dispositions to cry. *Melodious birds sing Madrigalls:—When as I sat in Pabilon: and a thousand vagram Posies. To shallow,* etc.
>
> *Sim.* Yonder he is comming, this way, Sir Hugh.
>
> *Evan.* Hee's welcome: *To shallow Rivers, to whose fals:* Heaven prosper the right: what weapons is he?

Marlowe's lyric was first printed in 1599. It was given its first musical setting in William Corkine's *Second Book of Ayres* (1612) where the music appears as one of his "Lessons for the Lyra Viol" (Fig. 5). The modern notation is taken from Chappell's *Popular Music of the Olden Time,* I, 215.[8] The tune may be older than the date of Corkine's book of ayres would indicate: a canto in Thomas Deloney's *Strange Histories* . . . (1607) is called "The Imprisonment of Queen Elinor, To the tune of Come live with me and be my love."[9]

FIGURE 5.—Come live with me and be my love

The line of the 137th Psalm could have had innumerable tunes for its setting. The composition of music to accompany the psalms was a pursuit which kept the musically inclined gentlemen of the period almost as busy as did the writing of sonnets. The setting shown in Figure 6 is taken from *Day's Psalter* (1583); the transcription is from Gibbon's *Melody and the Lyric,* p. 41. The 1602 Quarto version of *Merry Wives* gives in place of the psalm the line, *There dwelt a man in Babylon,* which is the beginning of the ballad "The goodly and constant wyfe Susanna." Apart from the similarity of the opening line, the ballad has no resemblance to the psalm. The Folio version seems more appropriate to the situation, however, especially since in it the accent of Sir Hugh is retained.

The most prominent use of music occurs in the little masque

When we did sit in Babylon The rivers round a- bout Then in remembrance of Si-on The
tears of grief burst out We hang'd our hearts and instruments The willow trees up-on For
in that place me for their use Had planted many one.

FIGURE 6.—Psalm 137

at the conclusion of the play (V, v). Since this scene contains the climax of the play and since it ties off the strands of the plot, we should note the contribution made by the music to the denouement. Here we may observe a finely wrought example of dramatic economy.

The device in which Falstaff is tormented by the fairies serves several functions, all of them contributing to the climax of the play. It serves as a culminating joke by which Falstaff is chastised, thus concluding the farcical strand of the plot, and it permits the romantic strand to be tied off in pantomime at the same time the mock fairies are scorching the lusty knight. Most of the music in the play is performed during this scene—an amount of music large enough to seem an exception to the opinion expressed earlier, that Shakespeare found farce and music uncongenial partners. How can this exception be explained?

In writing the scene, Shakespeare no doubt remembered earlier scenes from Lyly's play *Endimion* and from the anonymous *The Maydes Metamorphosis* in which mortals are surrounded and pinched by dancing fairies. As these two plays had been performed a little earlier by choirboy companies lately revived at St. Paul's and at Blackfriars, he may have discovered in this scene a chance to create humor at the expense of the singing boys who were enticing customers away from the playhouse of the Lord Chamberlain's Men. The introduction of singing boys into *The Merry Wives* would thus point up the resemblance between Shakespeare's scene and those of the choirboys.

Another clear result of the music in the scene is its use to sustain sound during the pantomime which it accompanies. The concluding song provides the only intelligible sound at this point of the play; Falstaff is groaning and yelping with pain and fright while Dr. Caius steals away the wrong person and Fenton carries off Anne—both actions done as a dumb show. The words and music of the fairy song thus preserve the aural interest of the audience without distracting attention from the pantomime.

As a final result we may note that the music underscores the climax of the play. We have earlier observed Shakespeare placing music at climactic points in his comedies. We thus find him following a practice which he had utilized frequently enough to be considered a pattern of dramatic technique.

The Quarto provides a description of the music and its performance in the scene. Just before the "fairies" enter, the Quarto stage directions state:

> *There is a noise of hornes, the two women run away.*
> *Enter Sir Hugh like a Satyre, and boyes dresst like*
> *Fayries, mistresse Quickly, like the Queene of Fayries:*
> *they sing a song about him, and afterward speake.*

We know very little about this first song. No lyric is given in any text, though that of the following song appears in the Folio text. Why is not the first song preserved? It may be that no well-defined song was performed at this point in the play. Possibly the song was actually a clamor of musical cries. Mistress Page, in outlining the prospective joke to her husband, plans to have the fairies "from forth a saw-pit rush at once/ With some diffused song." Hart, the Arden editor, accepts the word "diffused" as meaning "careless, irregular, wild." If so, perhaps there was no lyric worthy of preservation to accompany the entrance of the boy-fairies.

After Falstaff's trial by fire, Quickly proclaims:

> A little distant from him stand,
> And every one take hand in hand,
> And compasse him within a ring,
> First pinch him well, and after sing.[10]

We do not know what song was sung at this point in the Quarto version since no lyric was printed therein. Quickly's concluding lines in the masque describe the music as a roundel, that is, a circular dance-song. Very likely the song appearing in the Folio is the same as, or much like, the song omitted by the Quarto. Certainly the song in the Folio was written expressly for Shakespeare's scene.

After the children burn and pinch Falstaff, they form a ring around him and dance and sing this song:

The Song.

> *Fie on sinnefull phantasie: Fie on Lust and Luxurie:*
> *Lust is but a bloudy fire, kindled with unchaste desire,*

Fed in heart whose flames aspire,
As thoughts do blow them higher and higher.
Pinch him (Fairies) mutually: Pinch him for his villanie.
Pinch him, and burne him, and turne him about,
Till Candles, & Starlight, & Moone-shine be out.[11]

The musical setting originally used for this lyric is not known. It may have been as elaborate in form as the "Urchin's Dance" reproduced earlier,[12] or it may have been a simpler, syllabic setting. The latter would, perhaps, be more in keeping with the comic spirit of the play.

Though we do not have the original music for the song, there is an instrumental score in Antony Holborne's *Pavans, galliards, almains, and other short aeirs . . .* (1599) to which the lyrics can be set with relative ease. Holborne's tune is named, appropriately, "The Fairie-round." Shown in Figure 7 are the treble and bass parts transcribed in modern notation, to which has been set the fairy song from *The Merry Wives.*[13] The usual practice of composers in early instrumental forms was to embellish simple dance tunes with all sorts of variations; therefore, a vocal arrangement of Holborne's dance would probably have been simpler, thus permitting a closer fit of words to music, than the arrangement in the transcription.

The Quarto stage directions describe the action which accompanies the song:

Here they pinch him, and sing about him, & the
Doctor comes one way & steales away a boy in red,
And Slender another way he takes a boy in greene.
And Fenton steales misteris Anne, being in white.
And a noyse of hunting is made within: and
all the Fairies runne away. Falstaffe pulles
of his bucks head, and rises up. And enters
M. Page, M. Ford, and their wives, M. Shallow,
Sir Hugh.

We have considered the dramatic function of the song earlier, also its relationship to the action which it accompanies. There is one reference in the stage directions just quoted which now should be noted. We read therein that "a noyse of hunting is made within."

This was almost certainly a series of notes played on a hunting horn, the standard offstage signal for the hunt. When we recall that the entrance of the mock fairies is heralded by "a noise of hornes," it is apparent that the scene is introduced by the sound of hunting horns and closed in the same manner. The reference to Herne, the ghostly hunter, is clear. We can therefore better appreciate Falstaff's fear and bewilderment at the appearance of the fairies. He was doubtless expecting the spectral woodsman at any moment, especially since he had been prepared earlier to fear the great oak and its guardian.[14]

The horn player, in order to increase Falstaff's fright, probably

FIGURE 7.—Fie on sinnefull phantasie

chose the signal "The death of a Bucke with houndes" to introduce the fairies. To end the jest, the horn call "A strake of nyne, to draw home the companie" seems appropriate. Both of these hunting calls are taken from a complete set of hunting signals printed, with the musical notation, in George Turberville's *The Noble Arte of Venerie* . . . (1575), p. 251, "as are used here, in this noble Realme of England."

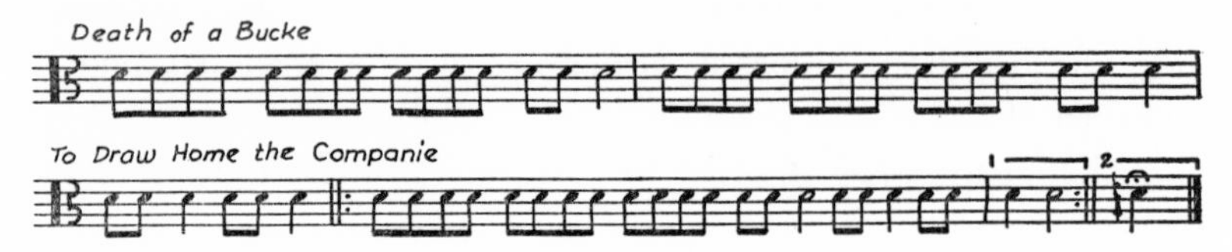

FIGURE 8.—The death of a Bucke
A strake of nyne

The use of the horn calls in this scene marks a recurrence of a standard device of Elizabethan dramatists—the use of music to introduce or accompany supernatural scenes or characters. In the earlier instances that we have observed in which this device was used, the music supplied was in most cases performed by an instrumental consort. In this scene, however, a consort would not have fitted the contemporary concept of probability. The episode occurs in the woods; the fairies are actually children; the jesters are middle-class citizens. In these circumstances the comparatively elaborate consort would be out of place, whereas the music of horns is appropriate to the setting and to the musical resources of the pranksters.

When we review the use of music in *The Merry Wives,* the efficiency with which it is used is impressive. The song snatches of Quickly and Sir Hugh indicate emotional turmoil in both cases: in the case of Sir Hugh this discomposure is made more comic than otherwise by his confusion of sacred and profane songs. The fairy roundel has diverse functions: it burlesques scenes from the choirboy plays; it supplies aural interest during the pantomime; and it underscores the climactic scene of the play. The horn calls which open and close the miniature masque furnish a musical frame for the episode and link the Herne legend more closely to the action of the play.

Notes

1. See J. Long, *Shakespeare's Use of Music,* I, 94, 95.
2. The text is that of the First Folio unless otherwise noted.
3. The use of birdcalls or whistles in the Elizabethan playhouses was no novelty. See W. Lawrence, *Pre-Restoration Stage Studies,* pp. 199-208.
4. Long, *op. cit., p.* 38.
5. I believe the Folio version of this scene is an occasional revision of the earlier, and more organic, Quarto version. See my discussion, "Another Masque for 'The Merry Wives of Windsor,'" *SQ,* III, 39-43.
6. First Folio text.
7. See Shakespeare, *Merry Wives,* Arden edition, XXIV, line 44 and Fn.
8. See also the reprint in E. Fellowes, *The English School of Lutenist Song Writers.*
9. Arden edition, XXIV, 111.
10. Q1602 text.
11. First Folio text.
12. See Long, *op. cit.,* I, 101.
13. "The Fairie-round" and "The Night Watch" are transcribed from the copy of Holborne's book in the Huntington Library.
14. See IV, iv, 28-45; V, i, 12, 13; V, v, 30, 31.

TWO

All's Well That Ends Well *and* *Measure for Measure*

ITH THESE TWO "BITTER" OR "PROBLEM" COMEdies, dated 1602-1603 and 1604 respectively, according to Sir E. K. Chambers' chronology, we enter what is considered by many a low plateau of artistic effort by Shakespeare.[1] Whether there is any significant connection between this opinion and the comparative lack of music in the two plays cannot be ascertained, but certainly there is a noticeable paucity of music in them if we compare these with either the preceding comedies or those following. There are only a few cornet flourishes and a march in *All's Well,* and one song in *Measure for Measure.* Despite this dearth of music performed in the two plays, several musical and dramatic incidents are worth consideration.

All's Well presents something quite new. For the first time in Shakespeare's plays all of the music seems to be performed by a band of cornets instead of by singers, or by the customary consort of strings or woodwinds, or by a combination of the two, commonly called by the general term "Musicke." Cornets are specifically named in the stage directions of I, ii and II, i, and they are the only instruments named by the Folio stage directions as actually sounding. Soldiers representing the army of the Duke of Florence appear on the stage with drum and trumpet (III, iii); the Widow mentions trumpets being heard (III, v, 1-9); and Lafeu speaks of the "King's . . . trumpets" (V, ii, 54-58); but no trumpets are named in the stage directions in these scenes as actually sounding, although some editors (Hardin Craig, for example) have added such directions. The explanation for this slight confusion may be found in the versatility of the cornetists and their instruments in imitating other instruments—trumpets in this case. The cornetists frequently supplied trumpet flourishes in plays by other dramatists of the period.[2] This practice might provide several exceptions to the rule established by W. J. Lawrence for the chronology of the later Shakespeare plays.[3]

Lawrence noted that the stage directions in plays produced around 1600 and shortly thereafter by the singing boys in the private playhouses almost always called for the music of cornets. The stage directions in the "public" plays, however, make little or no reference to the cornets. This, with other evidence, caused Lawrence to reason that those plays of Shakespeare containing references to cornets, or cornets and trumpets together, must have been written after 1609, or printed from prompt copies in use after 1609, when the King's Men took over the Blackfriars theater and, supposedly, the band of cornetists which furnished much of the music for the choirboy plays performed therein.

All's Well and John Marston's *The Malcontent,* performed by the King's Men in 1604, both call for the music of cornets, and of cornets only. They are, therefore, exceptions to Lawrence's general rule. It is possible that the Blackfriars cornetists were temporarily employed by the King's Men at the Globe, perhaps because of some reorganization of the Blackfriars boy company incidental to the death of Queen Elizabeth in 1603. In the center of all this conjecture, however, we may be reasonably certain that in 1603 or 1604 the King's Men employed a specific type of consort—the cornets.

Let us now turn to the episodes in which music is performed, considering first the ballad "Was this fair face the cause quoth she" (I, iii, 73-82). As noted by Dover Wilson and Sir Arthur Quiller-Couch, this may be a part of an old ballad entitled "The Lamentation of Hecuba and the Ladyes of Troy" whose text has been lost.[4] There is no indication in the Folio text that the clown sings these lines, although the singing of ballad snatches was traditionally a part of the clown's act. The actual performance of music at this point is hence debatable. Even so, we may still apply a structural analysis of the "Troy" stanzas which seem, in a manner other than the Countess suggests, corrupt.

If the lines are actually those of a ballad, they should be divisible into smaller units or stanzas than are shown in the text. The usual ballad stanza is short—four or six lines—in order to fit the simple tunes to which ballads were usually set. Also, the common custom was to use the same tune, merely repeated, for the successive stanzas of a particular ballad. This means that the stanzaic structure must not vary to any great extent. If we accept these postulates, a need for regularization appears in the first three lines of the ballad. Here is the text as it appears in the First Folio:

Was this fair face the cause, quoth she,
Why the Grecians sacked Troy,
Fond done, done, fond was this King Priams joy,
With that she sighed as she stood, bis
And gave this sentence then, among nine bad if one be good, among nine bad if one be good, there's yet one good in ten.

Obviously the compositor had trouble in setting the type for the ballad. He used a repeat sign after the fourth line, ran line five into line six, then repeated line six in full, running it into line seven. Haste or confusion is shown here, either in the manuscript or in the printing. Despite the confusion of the lines, the latter half of the stanza is easily regularized, thus:

With that she sighéd as she stood,
With that she sighéd as she stood,
And gave this sentence then,
Among nine bad if one be good,
Among nine bad if one be good,
There's yet one good in ten.

This stanza is of handy ballad length. If we may then assume that the preceding lines should be of like structure, we might write the stanza in this form:

Was this fair face the cause, quoth she,
Was this fair face the cause, quoth she,
Why the Grecians sackéd Troy?
Fond done, done, fond . . .
Fond done, done, fond . . .
Was this King Priam's joy?

The remainder of the fragmentary line is lost.

The music played by the cornets consists of several flourishes and tuckets, and a march. Flourishes are sounded at the entrance and exit of the King in I, i; for his entrance and exit in II, i and II, i, 23; and for the entrance of the Duke of Florence in III, i, and his exit in III, i, 23. A tucket sounds to indicate the approach of the triumphant Duke and his army in III, v. A change in the direction of the procession is shown by another tucket in the same scene, line 7. The near approach of the procession is indicated by the music of a march, line 40 of the scene. In V, ii, 54, an interlinear cue spoken by Lafeu calls for a tucket which is followed by a flourish at the beginning of the next scene for an entrance by the King. A final flourish ends the play. The use of musical signals to suggest off-stage movements of armies or processions, evidently well understood by Shakespeare's audience, provides a good example of one type of dramatic economy.

The distinction between the flourish and the tucket is quite clear. The flourish was quite ceremonious; it was an elaborate fanfare played by a choir of trumpets or cornets (four or five instruments). Usually the flourish was repeated three times.[5] The tucket, as Edward Naylor notes, was a personal trumpet call by which an individual or a noble family might be heralded.[6] It was almost always played on one instrument, a trumpet or cornet.

The notation of authentic trumpet calls, particularly the flourishes, of Shakespeare's time are very rare. The Royal Trumpeters did not play from musical notation, but transmitted their music by ear from father to son; hence, it is difficult to find any written record of the ceremonial trumpet fanfares. In Morley's *First Booke of Consort Lessons* (1599, 1611), however, is a trumpet march called "De la Tromba Pavin" which contains a trumpet flourish. Slightly abbreviated and transcribed for three B-flat trumpets and trombone, this passage is shown in Figure 9. Also shown in Figure 9 is an Italian cavalry tucket provided by E. Naylor, *Shakespeare and Music,* p. 202. The tucket is apparently as close as he could come to a Shakespearean version.

Military marches in Shakespeare's day were usually played by a fife and drums. In *All's Well,* as we have noted, there is no indi-

FIGURE 9.—Flourish and Tucket for Trumpets

cation in the stage directions that any instruments other than cornets are used; however, the cornet consort was quite capable of playing a march for the army of the Duke of Florence. No military marches scored specifically for cornets are known, at least none scored in Shakespeare's lifetime. We must therefore be contented with a lutenist's version of a military march found in Cambridge University Library (MS, D.d. 2.11 fol. 57r). This march, apparently recorded in the manuscript around the beginning of the seventeenth century, is shown in Figure 10.

* * * * * * * * * * *

Measure for Measure is likewise exceptional in its paucity of music. Other than the song, "Take, oh take those lips away," there is no performed music in the play. The one song, however, is intrinsically valuable, and it serves a definite dramatic purpose. Sir E. K. Chambers suggests that it might have been an interpolation for a Jacobean revival of the play.[7] Yet there are reasons for believing that the song was intentionally used by Shakespeare and that it is an integral part of the play and thus a part of the original manuscript.

FIGURE 10.—Military March

In considering the earlier comedies, we have noticed that Shakespeare was frequently influenced by references to music in the sources of his plays. When we turn to the principal source for this one, George Whetstone's *Promos and Cassandra* (1578), we find seven songs placed at intervals within the work. Of these, one is sung by Cassandra (V, vi).

> Sith fortune thwart, doth crosse my joyes with care,
> Sith that my blisse is chaungde to bale by fate:
> Sith frowarde chaunce, my dayes in woe doth weare,
> Sith I alas, must mone without a mate.
> I wretch have vowde, to sing both daye and night,
> O sorrowe staye, all motions of delight.
>
> Come grieflie griefe, torment this harte of mine,
> Come deepe dispaire, and stoppe my loathed breath,
> Come wretched woe, my thought of hope to pine:
> Come cruell care, preferre my sute to death.
> Death, end my wo, which sing both daye and night,
> O sorrowe slaye, all motions of delight.[8]

The melancholy tone of the song and the situation described by Cassandra form an obvious parallel to Shakespeare's song. The inference is strong that Whetstone's song suggested "Take, oh take those lips away."

While the song is being performed in *Measure for Measure,* Mariana is presented to the audience for the first time. The rejected lover of Angelo, she is shown grieving over the loss of his love.

Actus Quartus, Scoena Prima
Enter Mariana, and a Boy singing.

Song

Take, oh take those lips away,
that so sweetly were forsworne,
And those eyes: the breake of day,
lights that doe mislead the Morne
But my kisses bring againe, bring againe
Seales of love, but seal'd in vaine, seal'd in vaine.

Enter Duke

Mar. Breake off thy song, and haste thee quick away,
Here comes a man of comfort, whose advice
Hath often still'd my brawling discontent.
I cry you mercie, Sir, and well could wish
You had not found me here so musicall.
Let me excuse me, and beleeve me so,
My mirth it much displeas'd, but pleas'd my woe.
Duk. Tis good, though Musick of hath such a charme
To make bad good; and good provoake to harm.[9]

The dramatic function of the song seems to be aimed at an immediate characterization of Mariana upon her entry. The probability that she is an addition to Shakespeare's gallery of melancholics appears when we compare her remark about the music, it "pleas'd my woe," to Jaques' comment that he could "sucke melancholy out of a song, / As a Weazel suckes egges:" and to Duke Orsino's craving for sad music, "Give me excesse of it: that surfetting,/ The appetite may sicken, and so dye." Thus, from the effect of the song and knowledge previously given us of Mariana's plight, our sympathies are instantly drawn to her before she speaks a line.

The statements of Mariana and the Duke concerning the psychological effects of music are drawn from Renaissance musico-medical lore. She speaks of music as pleasing to her woe, that is, in her present state music increases her melancholy which, in turn, provides a type of pleasure. As one contemporary writer remarks:

For we know that life is as it were put into the deadst sorows by inflexion & modulation of voice. And they whose heartes even yearne for very greefe sometimes fall on singing not to seek comfort therein (for the best seeming comfort in such cases is to be comfortles) but rather to set the more on flote that pensiveness wherwith they are perplexed.[10]

The Duke, though, fears that too many applications of sad music may "provoake to harm." His warning is amplified by Robert Burton in *The Anatomy of Melancholy* (1621), pp. 374, 375:

As [music] is acceptable to most, so especially to a melancholy man. Provided alwaies, his disease proceed not originally from it, that he be not some light *inamorato,* some idle phantasticke, who capers in conceit all day long, and thinks of nothing else, but how to make Gigges, Sonnets, Madrigals in commendation of his Mistresse. In such cases Musicke is most pernitious, as a spurre to a free horse, it will make him runne himselfe blind or breake his wind, it will make such melancholy persons mad, and the sound of those Gigges & Horepipes, will not be removed out of their eares a weeke after.

This relationship of music and melancholy is perhaps best summed up by Sir Francis Bacon, who states succinctly, "But yet it hath been noted, that though this variety of tunes doth dispose the spirits to variety of passions, conform unto them, yet generally music feedeth that disposition of the spirits, which it findeth."[11]

The earliest musical setting of Mariana's song is a manuscript carrying the name of John Wilson in the Bodleian Library (MS Mus. b.l, fol. 19v). Other manuscript versions of Wilson's setting appear in the British Museum Addit. MS 11,608, fol. 56, and in the Drexel Collection of the New York Public Library. Two settings exist in the Drexel Collection: one, Drexel 4041 No. 44, is shown in Figure 11 and in the Appendix; the other is in Drexel 4257 (the Gamble Commonplace Book) No. 16. None of the manuscript versions are dated, but they seem to have been written between c. 1630 and c. 1650. Wilson's setting was first printed in

FIGURE 11.—Take, oh take those lips away

John Playford's *Select Musicall Ayres & Dialogues* (1653). Later, the song was printed in Wilson's *Cheerful Ayres and Ballads* (1660). It has since been reprinted in numerous books and collections of music. The version in Figure 11, however, is here published for the first time anywhere.

It is doubtful that John Wilson wrote his setting for Shakespeare's play. When *Measure for Measure* was first performed, John Wilson, or Dr. John Wilson, was a boy.[12] Of course, he may have been precocious, but early talent alone will not explain the additional stanza which appears in Wilson's settings, though not in the play lyrics.

> hide o hide those hils of snow
> which thy frosen bosome bares
> one whose tops the pinks that grow
> are of those that abrioll wares
> but first sett my poore hart free
> bound in icee chaines by the.[13]

Both stanzas—the first found in *Measure for Measure* and the second added by Wilson—are used in John Fletcher's *The Bloody Brother* (Q1639). The lyrics of Shakespeare's song are apparently directed at a male lover; the second stanza added by Fletcher and

Wilson indicates that their songs are directed at a lover's mistress. Moreover, Shakespeare's lyrics repeat the phrases "bring againe" and "seal'd in vaine," but the lyrics of Fletcher and Wilson omit these repetitions. It would seem, then, that either Fletcher borrowed Shakespeare's lyrics and added a second stanza, or Shakespeare used part of an anonymous song later used in its entirety by Fletcher. It also seems that Wilson wrote his setting for Fletcher's version, since he used Fletcher's arrangement of the lyrics.[14]

The musical setting of the song in *Measure for Measure* probably resembled closely that of Wilson. The lyrics call for a graceful, urbane ayre requiring a skilled singer—the singing boy mentioned in the stage direction. No instrumental group is named in the First Folio text, nor is the scene one wherein a consort is necessary. The accompaniment in this case was probably played on a lute by the singer.

The authorship of "Take, oh take those lips away" may be debatable, and John Wilson may not have composed his setting for Shakespeare's song specifically; yet, in its genesis and dramatic application in *Measure for Measure,* the song has Shakespeare's mark on it, and Wilson's setting is charming and appropriate.

Notes

1. *William Shakespeare,* I, 451-453. See also W. A. Neilson and C. J. Hill, *Complete Plays and Poems of William Shakespeare,* pp. 354, 390; W. J. Craig, *The Complete Works of Shakespeare,* pp. 803, 833.
2. The varied uses of the cornets in plays may be seen in J. Marston's *Antonio and Mellida, Sophonisba, The Fawn,* as well as in *The Malcontent.*
3. *Shakespeare's Workshop,* pp. 48-74.
4. *All's Well,* New Cambridge edition, pp. 128, 129.
5. For a more extensive discussion of the flourish see C. Titcomb, "Baroque Court and Military Trumpets . . . ," *The Galpin Society Journal,* IX, 56-81.
6. *Shakespeare and Music,* pp. 174, 175.
7. *Op. cit.,* I, 455.
8. *THE RIGHT EXCEL-/lent and famous Historye, . . .* Folger Shakespeare Library.
9. First Folio text.
10. J. Barnes, *The Praise of Musicke . . . ,* p. 34.
11. *Works . . . ,* II, Cent. ii, 26.

12. The most recent discussion of the identity of John Wilson and his relationship with Shakespeare may be found in P. Seng, *The Dramatic Function of the Songs . . .*, pp. 463 ff.
13. Text from New York Public Library MS. Drexel 4041. See Appendix.
14. For additional discussion of this subject see Seng, *op. cit.;* R. Noble, *Shakespeare's Use of Song,* pp. 89, 91; E. Reed, *Songs from the British Drama,* p. 280.

THREE

The Cosmic Gamut

EFORE WE TURN TO THE LAST FOUR OF SHAKE-speare's comedies—*Pericles, Cymbeline, The Winter's Tale,* and *The Tempest*—we should survey briefly the place of music in Renaissance cosmology. This diversion is necessary if we are to comprehend better Shakespeare's use of music in these plays because in them he usually assigns to the performed music a symbolic function. Shakespeare uses music to express one aspect of the Neo-Platonic world-view so prominent in Renaissance thought. Walter C. Curry has examined some of the elements of Neo-Platonism as he perceived them in *The Tempest,* but his study did not include music as one of these elements.[1] A few excerpts from the writings of four contemporaries of Shakespeare should give us at least an elementary understanding of Music as a cosmic concept familiar to many Elizabethans and, therefore, a concept of great symbolic value.

The cosmology of many educated Elizabethans was to a great extent based on musical concepts derived largely from Pythagoras, Plato, and Plotinus, as syncretized by later philosophers, notably Boethius and Polydor Virgil. The development of the idea of World Harmony has been traced very ably by Leo Spitzer;[2] hence, we need not attempt here what has been previously well done. We shall note, however, some additional expressions of this world-view which should leave little doubt that Shakespeare's use of music for symbolic purposes was an example not only of a general practice of Elizabethan writers, but of a practice widely understood by their readers. Lorenzo's apostrophe to music in *The Merchant of Venice,* V, as well as the musical symbolism in the final comedies we are to examine, originated in a contemporary rationale considerably more systematic than poetic.

The concept of order and degree in the universe, as symbolized by the musical scale, is graphically illustrated by M. Mersenne in his *Traité de L'Harmonie Universelle* (1627), p. 87. There appears the table reproduced below.

Mersenne's Gamut

ff	Dieu le Pere	10	Seraphim	Amour de Dieu.
ee	Le Fils	20	Cherubin	Intelligence.
cc	Le S. Esprit	30	Thrones	Entendement.
bb	Mens	40	Dominations	Amour du prochain.
aa	L'entendemēt	50	Principautez	Raison
gg	La raison	60	Puissances	Haine de soy mesme.
f	La volonté	70	Vertus	Haine du monde.
e	Saturne	80	Archanges	Imagination
d	Iupiter	90	Anges	Sentiment
c	Mars	100	Premier mobile	Volonté.
b	Le Soleil	200	Firmament	Action.
a	Venus	300	♄	Faculté recevante.
g	Mercure	400	♃	Faculté naturelle.
F	La Lune	500	♂	Irascible.
E	Le feu	600	☉	Vitale.
D	La supréme (regiō de l'air)	770	♀	Concupiscible.
C	La moyenne	800	☿	Phantastique.
B	L'inférieure	900	☽	Vegetante.
A	L'eau	1000		
G	La terre	2000		

Moving left to right, the first column shows the gamut, or musical scale, in ascending notes. The second column presents the corresponding order of the universe (based on the Ptolemaic system). Mathematical (numerological) correspondences appear in the third column. In the fourth is the analogous hierarchy of terrestrial, aerial, and angelic spirits (associated with astrology, alchemy, sorcery, and magic, both black and white). The final column provides the corresponding "faculties" of the animate creatures of the world. As may be observed, Mersenne's gamut is here associated closely with a modified Platonic Ladder of Love, or, in Christian terms, a Jacob's Ladder reaching from the depths of vasty hell to the "young-eyed cherubins" and thence to God, the Father.

Mersenne's system is mainly Neo-Platonic, though adapted to

a Roman Catholic theology and expressed in a thoroughly scholastic form and terminology. He divides Music into four general categories, in a descending order of spirituality. The first category is "La Musique Divine, ou Archetype, de qui dépend la nostre, est dans l'intellect divin: elle est Interieure ou Exterieure, & a pour son objet tout ce qui est sujet aux proportions harmoniques, & tout ce qui en est capable."[3] The second category he terms "La Musique creée [qui] est dépendante de la Divine, & se peut diviser en autant de parties comme il y a d'especes au monde. laquelle n'est autre chose que l'ordre & la proportion harmonique qui se trouve entre les parties du monde, & de chaque individu en particulier."[4]

The third and fourth categories are those which provided Shakespeare and his contemporaries throughout Western Europe with seminal concepts, figurative language, and the symbols that poets and dramatists were to find invaluable. In Mersenne's words, "La Musique Mondaine est l'ordre & proportion harmonique & agreable a l'entendment, laquelle se trouve dans la fabrique des Cieux & des Elemens, & dans leurs proprietez & mouvemens," and "La Musique Humaine est le rapport des humeurs, & des parties du corps, des facultez de l'ame, & de ses actions comparées les unes avec les autres."[5] It is in the concept of "La Musique Mondaine" that the ideas of the music of the spheres and the power of music to control the elemental matter and forces—calm tempests, erect cities, tame animals and fish—are set forth. And it is in the concept of "La Musique Humaine" that the association of musical harmony with the "humors" of the body gives rise to all sorts of medical and psychological lore based on the effects of the harmonious or inharmonious tuning of the four humors within the physical body of a human being.

A work similar to Mersenne's *Traité,* though it lacks the detail and carefully skirts theological questions, is Joseph Barnes' *The Praise of Musicke* (1586). Barnes, for the most part, restricts his discussion to *musica mundana* and *musica humana,* but the Neo-Platonic concepts are no less evident. He states his world-view briefly and succinctly; "For time canōt say that hee was before her [Music], or nature that she wrought w^t^out her. To prove this looke upon the frame & workmanship of the whole worlde, whether there be not above, an harmony between the spheares, beneath a simbolisme between the elements. Looke upon a man, who the Philosophers termed a little world, whether the parts accord not one to the other by consent and unity."[6]

In his account of *musica mundana* Barnes provides a discussion of the music of the spheres which, because it is brief and to the point, may be quoted in full.

Pithagoras and his sectatours, thought that the world did not consist without musical proportion and concent. And therefore both he & the best philosophers ascribe unto every Celestial sphere, one *Goddess* or Muse, which is the governes & ruler thereof: & because there are eight of those spheres, the seven planets, and the eight which is called the firmament, therefore they made 8. peculiar Muses, attributing to *Luna* the muse *Clio:* to *Mercurius, Euterpe:* to *Venus, Thalia:* to *Sol, Melpomene:* to *Mars, Terpsichore:* to *Jupiter, Erato:* to *Saturne, Polymnia,* to the firmamēt or *coleum stellarum, Urania;* and because of eight particular soundes or voices, keeping due proportion and time, must needs arise an harmony or concent, which is made by them all, therefore that sound which al these make is called *Calliope.* And hence is that pleasant harmony of the celestial globes caused, which *Pythagoras* so much speaketh of. If then both Gods and men, and unreasonable creatures of what kind soever, be allured and mitigated with musicke, we may safely conclude that this proceedeth from that hidden virtue, which is between our soules and musicke: and be bold with *Pindarus* to affirme, that . . . Al those things that *Jupiter* doth not love, do only contemne the songs of the Muses.[7]

To describe other powers of *musica mundana,* Barnes repeats the legend of Arion.

Arion seeing no way to escape the furie of his cruel enemies, tooke his *Citterne* in his hand, and to his instrument sang his last song, where-with not only the dolphins flocked in multitudes about the ship readie to receive him on their backes, but even the sea that rude and barbarous element, being before rough and tempestuous, seemed to allay his choler, waxing calme on a sodaine, as if it had beene to give *Arion* quiet passage through the waves.[8]

In writing of *musica humana,* Barnes quotes Giraldus, who in turn draws from Plato and the Neo-Platonists to establish a relationship, sufficiently firm by medieval standards, between Music and the human psyche. Those familiar with Plato's *Republic* will recognize the described tripartite division of the soul:

The symphony & concent of Musicke . . . agreeth with the interior parts & affections of the soule. For as there are three partes or faculties of mans soule, the first and worthiest the part *reasonable,* which is ever chiefe, & never in subiectiō to the other, the second *irascible,* which, as it is ruled of the former, so ruleth the latter, and the last *cōcupiscible,* which ever obeith, & never ruleth; so if we cōpare the symphony of Musicke, with these powers of the soule, we shal find great conveniencie and an affinity between them. For looke what proportion is betweene the parts *reasonable,* & *irascible,* such is there in Musicke between that string which is called *hypate,* & that which is termed *Mese,* causing the melody called *diatessaron:* and look what proportion is between *Mese* & *Nete* making that sound which is named *Diapente:* so that as those three partes of the soule consenting in one, make an absolute and perfect action: so of these three in Musicke, is caused a pleasant and delectable *Diapason.*[9]

Mersenne, in his more detailed discussion, develops, with considerable debt to Aristotle's *Ethics,* an association of the humane music of the soul with a harmony of the intellectual virtues and moral virtues, in which Truth is the object of the first, and Right Action the object of the second. He remarks:

Premierement, il est certain que l'entendment est une faculté de l'ame raisonnable, ou de la nature spirituelle, telle qu'est l'Angelique & la Divine, qui a la verité pour son objet. Secondement, l'entendement humain ne peut de soy-mesme connoistre aucune verité, ny se joindre à son objet sans l'aide de quelque lumiere exterieure, ou de quelque qualité interieure; car au mesme instant qu'il est infus dans le corps avec l'ame raisonnable, il est semblable a la carte blanche qui n'a jamais receu aucun lineament. En troisieme lieu, l'entendement se sert de ses actes & de ses operations pour venir a la connoissance de son objet, & acquiert de certaines dispositions & habitudes sont appelées *vertus intellectuelles,* car comme la volonte recoit sa perfection des vertus morales, qui sont qu'elle a une grand inclination a son propre objet qui est le bien-honneste, de mesme les vertus intellectuelles donnent une grande inclination a l'entendment vers son objet qui est la merité.[10]

For a discussion of the medical and psychological lore associated with music in Shakespeare's day, we can probably do no better than to quote from Burton's *The Anatomy of Melancholy* (1621).

Many and sundry are the meanes, which Philosophers & Physitians have prescribed to exhilerate a sorrowful heart, to divert those fixed and intent cares and meditations, which in this malady so much offend; but in my Iudgment none so present, none so powerfull, none so apposite as a cup of strong drinke, mirth, Musick, and merry company. *Ecclus. 40.20. Wine and Musicke reioyce the heart. Rhasis cont. 9. Tract, 15. Altomarus cap. 7. Ælianus Montaltus cap. 26. Ficinus, Bened. Victor. Faventinus,* are almost immoderate in the commendation of it, a most forcible medicine, *Iacchinus* cals it. *Iason Pratensis, a most admirable thing, and worthy of consideration, that can so mollifie the Mind, and stay those tempestuous affections of it. Musica est mentis medicina masta,* a roaring-meg against Melancholy, to ereare and revive the languishing Soule, *affecting not only the eares, but the very arteries, the vitall and the animall spirits, it erects the mind, & makes it nimble. Lemnius instit. cap. 44.* And this it will effect in the most dull, severe, and sorrowfull Soules, *expell griefe with mirth, and if there be any cloudes or dust, or dregs of cares yet lurking in our thoughts, most powerfully it wipes them all away. Salisbur. polic. lib. 1. cap. 6.* and that which is more, it will performe all this in an instant. *Cheare up the countenance, expell austerity, bring in hilarity (Girald. Camb. cap. 12. Topog. Hiber.) informe our manners, mitigate anger; Athenaus Dipnosophist lib. 14. cap. 10.* calleth it, an infinite treasure to such as are indowed with it. *Dulcisonum resicit tristis corda melos, Eobanus Hessus.* Many other properties *Cassiodorus epist. 4.* reckons up of this our divine Musick, not only to expell the greatest griefes, but it *doth extenuate feares and furies, appeaseth cruelty, awakeneth heavinesse, and to such as are watchfull, it causeth quiet rest, it takes away splene and hatred,* and cures all irksomnesse and heavinesse of the Soule: laboring men that sing to their work, can tell as much, and so can souldiers when they goe to fight, who terror of death cannot so much affright, as Musick animates. *It makes a child quiet,* the nurses song &c. In a word it is so powerful a thing, that it ravisheth the Soule, and carries it beyond itself, helpes, elevates, extends it. *Scaliger exercit. 302.* gives a reason of these effects, *because the spirits about the Heart, take in that trembling and dancing aire into the Body, &c are moved together, & stirred up with it,* or els the mind, as some suppose, harmonically composed, is rowsed up at the tunes of Musicke. And t'is not only men that are affected with it, but almost all other creatures. You know the tale of *Orpheus,* that could *saxa movere sono testudinis* &c. make stocks and stones as well as beasts, other animals dance after his pipe. *Arion* that made fishes follow him, which as common experience evinceth, are much affected with Musick. All singing birds are much pleased with it, especially nightingales, if we may believe *Calcagninus,* and bees among the rest, though they be flying away, when they heare any tinkling sound, will tarry behind. *Harts, hinds, horses, dogges, beares are exceedingly delighted with it, Scal. exerc.* 302. Elephants *Agrippa* addes *lib.* 2 *cap.* 24. and in *Lidia* in the midst of a lake there be certain floating Ilands, that after good Musick will dance. But to leave all declamatory speeches in praise of divine Musick, I will confine my self to my proper subiect: besides that excellent power it hath to expell many other diseases, it is a soveraigne remedy against Despaire and Melancholy, and will drive away the Divell himselfe. *Canus* a Rhodian Fidler in *Philostratus,* when *Appollonius* was inqusitive to know what he could do with his pipe, told him, *that he could make a melancholy man merry, & him that was merry much merrier then before, a lover more inamored, a Religious man more divine. Chyron* the *Centaure* is said to have cured this and many other Diseases by Musick alone: as now they doe those, saith *Bodine,* that are troubled with *St. Vitus* bedlam dance. *Timotheus* the musician compelled *Alexander* to skip up & down, & leave his dinner (like the tale of the Friar & the Boy) whom *Austin de civ. dei lib. 17. c. 14.* so much commends for it. Who hath not heard how *Davids* harmony drove away the evill spirits frō King *Saul.* 1. *Sam.* 16. and *Elisha* when hee was much troubled by importunate Kings, called for a Minstrell, and *when hee plai'd the hand of the Lord came upon him,* 2. *Kings,* 3. *Iason Pratensis cap. de Mania* hath many examples, how *Clinias* and *Empedocles* cured some desparately melancholy, and some mad by musick alone. And because it hath such excellent vertues, belike *Homer* brings in *Phemius* playing, and the *Muses* singing at the banquet of the Gods. The *Greekes* & *Romans,* and all civill commonwealths have graced Musicke, & made it one of the liberall sciences, all Princes and Emperours, and persons of any quality, maintaine it in their Courts; No mirth without Musicke. Sir Thomas Moore in his absolute *Utopian* commonwealth, allowes Musick as an appendix to every meale, and that throughout to all sorts. *Lewes the xi* when he invited *Edward the 4.* to come to Paris, told him that as a principall entertainement, he should heare sweet voices of children, exquisite musicke, he should have a .... and the Cardinall of *Burbon* to be his Confessor, which he used as a most plausible argument: as to a sensuall man, indeed it is. *Scaliger* of himselfe ingeniously confesseth, *exercit.* 274. *I am beyond all measure affected with Musicke, I doe most willingly behold them dance, and am nightely detained & allured with that grace and comelinesse of faire women, and I am well pleased to be idle amongst them.* And what young man is not? As it is acceptable to most, so especially to a melancholy man. . . . Otherwise, saith *Plutarch, Musica magis dementat quam vinum.* Musicke makes some men mad: like *Astolphos* horne in *Ariosto:* and *Theophrastus* right well prophecied, that diseases were either made by Musicke, or mittigated.[11]

For a view of music less marked by appeals to classical unnatural history, and perhaps drawn from more direct observation, a few comments by Sir Francis Bacon are pertinent. In regard to the effects of music on the dispositions and humors of men, he is content to observe that "generally music feedeth that disposition of the spirits, which it findeth."[12] He then advances a "scientific" explanation for the popularity of the serenade and the aubade.

Sounds are meliorated by the intension of the sense, where the common sense is collected most to the particular sense of hearing, and the sight suspended: and therefore sounds are sweeter, as well as greater, in the night than in the day; and I suppose they are sweeter to blind men than to others: and it is manifest, that between sleeping and waking, when all the senses are bound and suspended, music is far sweeter than when one is fully waking.[13]

Lest this sequence of quotations on what Burton called "our divine Musicke" conclude in anticlimax, let us note, once more, Shakespeare's transmutation of many of the ideas we have encountered. Act V of *The Merchant of Venice* contains a summary which is also a beautiful example of poetic distillation.

Lor. How sweet the moone-light sleepes upon this banke,
Heere will we sit, and let the sounds of musicke
Creepe in our eares soft stilnes, and the night
Become the tutches of sweet harmonie:
Sit *Iessica,* looke how the floore of heaven
Is thicke inlayed with pattens of bright gold,

There's not the smallest orbe which thou beholdst
But in his motion like an Angell sings,
Still quiring to the young eyed Cherubins;
Such harmonie is in immortall soules,
But whilst this muddy vesture of decay
Doth grosly close in it, we cannot heare it . . .

Iessi. I am never merry when I heare sweet musique.

Play musicke.

Lor. The reason is, your spirits are attentive:
For doe but note a wilde and wanton heard
Or race of youthful and unhandled colts,
Fetching mad bounds, bellowing and neighing loud,
Which is the hot condition of their bloud,
If they but heare perchance a trumpet sound,
Or any ayre of musicke touch their eares,
You shall perceive them make a mutuall stand,
Their savage eyes turn'd to a modest gaze,
By the sweet power of musicke: therefore the Poet
Did faine that *Orpheus* drew trees, stones,
and floods.
Since naught so stockish, hard, and full of rage,
But musicke for the time doth change his nature,
The man that hath no musicke in himselfe,
Nor is not moved with concord of sweet sounds,
Is fit for treasons, stratagems, and spoyles,
The motions of his spirit are dull as night,
And his affections darke as *Erobus,*
Let no such man be trusted: marke the musicke.[14]

It is, of course, difficult to determine how much of the musical cosmology sketched above Shakespeare personally believed. But it cannot be denied that he was familiar with it, nor that he frequently drew upon it for figurative and symbolic purposes. Therefore, when we turn to the remaining comedies, we shall observe those episodes containing performed music with an eye to their symbolic values as well as to other dramatic functions; we shall seek for symbolic statements within a rationale generally understood, if not always believed, by the educated men of Shakespeare's time.

Notes

1. *Shakespeare's Philosophical Patterns.*
2. "Classical and Christian Ideas of World Harmony," *Traditio,* II, 409-464, and III, 307-364.
3. *Traité de L'Harmonie Universelle,* Théorème XIII.
4. *Ibid.,* Théorème XIV.
5. *Ibid.,* Théorèmes XV and XVI.
6. *The Praise of Musicke,* p. 2.
7. *Ibid.,* pp. 52, 53.
8. *Ibid.,* p. 49.
9. *Ibid.,* pp. 44, 45.
10. Mersenne, *op. cit.,* p. 13.
11. R. Burton, *Anatomy . . . ,* pp. 372-375.
12. Bacon, *Works . . . ,* II, 26.
13. *Ibid.,* p. 39.
14. First Folio text.

FOUR

Pericles

ITH *Pericles* WE MOVE FROM THE SHADOWS OF the two preceding "bitter" comedies into the warm sunset of the final comedies—the serious romances whose unifying theme of separation and reconciliation reaches its full realization in *The Tempest.* With the turning, or returning, of Shakespeare to a type of comedy more lyrical than *All's Well* and *Measure for Measure,* we might also expect the musical devices used by him in his earlier comedies to reappear. Nor shall we be disappointed; in these final romances a revival of poetic power is paralleled by an increasing use of music.

As far as the background information for this study is concerned, let us assume that the entire play is by Shakespeare. While we should not overlook the possibility that parts of the play, particularly the first two acts, may be from another hand, the evidence to this effect is not conclusive. Therefore, the date and sources of the play, as generally agreed upon, will form the basis for its examination here.

The Blount entry in the Stationers' Register in 1608 provides the earliest record of the play, although a play called *Pericles* was performed in London between 1606 and 1608.[1] The authoritative text is that of the first Quarto of 1609, an ill-printed, possibly stolen, version of the play.[2] The two principal sources are "Apollonius of Tyre" from Gower's *Confessio Amantis,* and a prose work, *The patterne of Painfull Adventures* (1576), by Lawrence Twyne, which was reprinted in 1607.[3]

Pericles seems to be essentially allegorical, even as a drama. The author seems to have made a conscious effort to imitate the interlude or morality play of an earlier age. The language assigned Gower, as Chorus, is archaic; the use of the dumb show, though apparently modified, is a reversion to an earlier dramatic style; and the straggling action of the play lacks the unity of the kind present in *Othello* or *Macbeth,* though it resembles the early sixteenth century interludes in this respect. If we consider the play as allegory, then it reveals a procession of personified virtues, both masculine and feminine. In the court of King Antiochus, Pericles is tested and triumphs through courage and faith. He is tested again at the court of King Simonides where he emerges triumphant in the courtly virtues of tilting, music, dancing, and love. In the following tempest his faith in Providence is tested by means of the apparent loss of his wife at sea and long separation from his daughter. The virtue of wisdom and practical skill is personified by Cerimon, the physician; chastity and the graceful arts by Marina. The combination of all these virtues finally results in the reuniting of Pericles with his wife and daughter and his Job-like recognition that the pattern of painful tests was only a seeming evil necessary for his recognition of a divine truth.

Throughout this allegorical structure there runs a prominent theme, the falsity of appearance or "fancy." Pericles, by means of a riddle, sees through the false and polluted love represented by the daughter of King Antiochus. When he appears at the court of King Simonides, his true nobility is disguised by his rough clothing and rusty armor, and he must show his "noblesse" by his acts. His genuine virtues are recognized by the King and Thaisa in spite of his external appearance, and he is rewarded with the hand of Thaisa in marriage—the true love as opposed to the false love of the princess of Antioch. When Thaisa, apparently dead, is cast upon the shore and is discovered and brought to Cerimon, he is able, by reason of his wisdom and skill, to restore her to life from seeming death. Upon discovery of his long-lost daughter and wife, Pericles finds joy where it seemed he had nothing to live for. Such examples of the falseness of fancy, or of judgments based upon superficial appearance, could be multiplied with little effort.

But what about the music in the play? It appears to be used to suggest or to emphasize several concepts with which, as we have previously noted, music was then closely associated: music accompanies the perception of a metaphysical Truth despite its physical disguises, Truth being perhaps synonymous with Mersenne's divine

Entendement; music symbolizes the social harmony between men (love of humanity) or between man and woman (marriage); music is a most sovereign remedy for despondence and is even capable of restoring life to the dead.

The first scene employing music is that in which Pericles interprets the riddle of King Antiochus. After stating the terms of the contract, the King calls for his daughter to appear. "Musicke bring in our daughter, clothed like a bride. . . ."[4] Presumably the music sounds as the princess appears and ceases when she leaves the stage.

There are several possible reasons why music is used at this point in the play. It might underscore the sensuous beauty of the King's daughter, speaking for her, in a sense, as she is given almost no speech in the play. The music might provide a point of reference for Pericles' description of the princess, after he has interpreted the riddle, as "a fair viol, and your sense the strings; . . . Hell only danceth at so harsh a chime." Here is also one of those crucial moments which, as we have noted earlier, Shakespeare usually underscored with music.[5] Yet all these possibilities may be comprehended in one musical symbol. In this case, however, the music symbolizes not a harmony of human love, but a dissonance resulting from a perversion of human love.

This scene provides an interesting parallel to Spenser's Bower of Acrasia, in which sensual love is surrounded by the music of Nature—singing birds, rippling brooks, murmuring leaves of the forest, amorous songs sung by wanton boys, and the bass notes of a waterfall. But since this sensual music is entirely worldly it is essentially false, as is the love of Acrasia. Likewise, the daughter of Antiochus is "clothed like a bride," "apparell'd like the spring," "Her face the book of praises," "the fruit of yon celestial tree" to be tasted, "Her face, like heaven," but not heavenly.[6] Her sense is the viol to whose strings "Hell only danceth at so harsh a chime." And she appears surrounded by the sound of music. Obviously, the music performed here should symbolize the sensuality and falsity of the love offered to Pericles.

We do not know, of course, what piece of music was performed on Shakespeare's stage at this point of the play, but we may suppose that it was marked by a pleasing and insinuating sweetness. The music was probably played by a broken consort of strings and woodwinds, the type of ensemble Frederick Sternfeld finds especially appropriate for amorous and wanton music.[7] A fitting score might be the tune "Light o' Love" shown in Figure 12, whose setting is taken from William Ballet's Lute Book (1594) as transcribed by J. Gibbon, *Melody and the Lyric . . .*, p. 54.

FIGURE 12.—Light o' Love

The court of King Simonides is quite different from that of Antiochus, although there Pericles again submits to a series of tests in an effort to win for wife the gracious Thaisa. These tests, however, are marked by a friendliness and nobility far removed from the atmosphere of Antiochus' court. The tests involve contests in chivalry —tilting, dancing, music, and courtly love.

King Simonides tests the suitors in their mastery of the gentler masculine skills, among them music and dancing. In this connection the strong influence of the sources of the play, as well as Shakespeare's departure from them, may be observed in the two scenes. In Twyne's version, the banquet and tilting follow the wedding of Apollonius and Lucina, of which he writes:

> And after dinner of the exquisite Musicke, fine dauncing, heavenly singing, sweete devising, and pleasant communication among the estates? I may not discourse at large of the liberall challenges made and proclaimed at the tilt, barriers, running at the ring, ioco di can, managing fierce horses, running a foote and dauncing in armour.[8]

Preceding the wedding, both Gower and Twyne describe a musical contest between Lucina and Apollonius. Shakespeare omits this contest, though he refers to it later in the play (II, v, 24-30) as having taken place. Twyne's account states:

Then saide the king unto his daughter: Madame I pray you take your harpe into your handes, and play us some musike to refresh our guests withal.[9]

Lucina plays, and all praise her skill but Apollonius. The King rebukes him:

You are too blame Apollonius, since all praise my daughter for her excellencie in musike, and you commend not her. Apollonius answered: My soveraine . . . she is not yet come to perfection in musike. For proofe whereof, if it please your grace to command the harp to be delivered unto me, she shal well perceive, that she shal heare that which she doth not yet know. The king answered: . . . I pray you take the harpe, and let us heare some part of your cunning. When Apollonius had received the harp, he went forth, and put a garland of flowers upon his head, and fastened his raiment in a comely manner about him, and entred into the parlour againe, playing before the king, and the residue with such cunning and sweetness, that he seemed rather to be Apollo than Apollonius, and the kings guests confessed that in al their lives they never heard the like before. But when Lucina had heard and seene what was done, she felt hir selfe sodainely mooved within, and was sharpelie surprised with the love of Apollonius. . . .[10]

The changes made by Shakespeare are significant. He shifts the "dauncing in armour" from the tourney (II, ii) to the banquet (II, iii); he omits the musical contest between Apollonius and Lucina, replacing it with what seems to be a duet dance performed by Pericles and Thaisa; and he places the events of II, ii before, rather than after, the wedding of Pericles and Thaisa. An obvious explanation of these alterations is the need for dramatic economy; but there are other interesting reasons.

Shakespeare evidently wanted the dance of the knights to be the culminating test before Pericles claims the hand of Thaisa. The musical bout between Apollonius and Lucina, which in the Twyne version displayed the hero's skill, would be out of place in the symbolism of the play since it would have placed Pericles and Thaisa, both symbols of good, in opposition. Hence, the knight's dance, showing Pericles in contest with the other suitors, provides the opportunity for Pericles to display his grace and thus to win Thaisa.

This interpretation becomes clearer if we consider the way in which both dances in the scene were originally staged. We shall have to reconstruct this scene afresh, as it has provoked a general misunderstanding on the part of many editors of the play.[11]

If we turn to the Q1609 text we find the following:

Enter the King and Knights from Tilting.

* * * *

King. . . . Come Gentlemen, we sit too long on trifles,
And waste the time which lookes for other revels?
Even in your Armours as you are addrest,
Will well become a Souldiers daunce:
I will not have excuse with saying this,
Lowd musike is too harsh for Ladyes heads,
Since they love men in Armes, as well as beds.

Most editors have added stage directions indicating that knights and ladies perform this and the following dance.[12] There is little dramatic reason for the presence of more than one lady in the scene, and many reasons why others should not be there. We are told that the King and Knights come on the stage from tilting. Thaisa is also present, because she speaks during the scene; but there is no evidence of other ladies appearing. The knights dance, true, but their dance is strictly a masculine affair. In the Twyne version, we remember, the dance was a part of the tourney in which only the knights engaged. The King describes the dance as a "Souldiers daunce." Clearly, the dance was a military one, probably of the same type as that described in Peele's *Arraignment of Paris,* wherein a stage direction (II, ii) states, *Hereupon enter Nine Knights treading a warlike almain, by drum and fife.*[13]

FIGURE 13.—Mounsieurs Almaine

For actual performance the producer might well follow Peele and use the instrumentation he calls for, the military drum and fife. In T. Morley's *First Book of Consort Lessons* (1599) is an almain suitable for this occasion, "Mounsieurs Almaine" No. 15. The treble viol part is transcribed in Figure 13.

At the completion of this dance King Simonides has reached a decision. He chooses Pericles from among the knights and presents him to Thaisa for the next dance. There is no mention of other ladies performing this dance, or of the knights taking any part in it. Here we have a duet dance between Pericles and Thaisa which symbolizes both Pericles' victory and his union with Thaisa. The dance ends with the two clasping hands. The King calls, "Unclasp, unclasp"; then, turning to the other knights, says, "Thanks, gentlemen, to all; all have done well,/But [to Pericles] you the best."[14]

A dance more graceful than the almain seems necessary in this case. The galliard seems more appropriate; therefore, in Figure 14

FIGURE 14.—Galliard

appears a galliard taken from Holborne's *Pavans, galliards, almains, and other short aeirs* (1599).

The possible reasons for Shakespeare's departure from his sources may now be brought into clearer focus. He perhaps changed the action to conform with the allegorical symbolism we have earlier observed. That is, the dance of the knights and its music symbolize the harmony, competitive but chivalric, of King Simonides' court as opposed to the false harmony of the court of King Antiochus. Likewise, the duet dance of Pericles and Thaisa symbolizes their true love as opposed to the incest-tainted love of the princess of Antioch.

The next test of Pericles is an ordeal designed to measure his patience in adversity. When he hears of Thaisa's death, he exclaims bitterly (III, i, 23-27): "O you gods!/ Why do you make us love your goodly gifts,/ And snatch them straight away? We here below/ Recall not what we give, and therein may/ Use honor with you." He is soon reconciled to divine will and comments, "Now, the good gods/ Throw their best eyes upon't!" He places Thaisa's body in a waterproof casket which is thrown into the sea. When Cerimon discovers the body of Thaisa, he calls for music as an aid in restoring her to life (Q1609-1): "The rough and Wofull Musick that we have, cause it to sound beseech you:/ The Violl once more: how thou stirrest thou block?/ The Musick their: I pray you give her ayre: . . ." And to the sound of the viol Thaisa awakens.

This episode is not in Twyne nor in Gower. Shakespeare is reflecting, we may suppose, the Renaissance belief in the animating power of music. We recall Burton's statement, ". . . *the spirits about the Heart, take in that trembling and dancing aire into the Body, &c are moved together, & stirred up with it.*"[15] Benedick puts it more concisely, if humorously, when he exclaims, "Is it not strange that sheeps' guts should hale souls out of men's bodies?" Or back in, we might add. It is the viol, as well as the suggested vial, that holds Cerimon's miraculous cure.[16]

The music sounds immediately upon Cerimon's command, line 88, and one passage is apparently completed before his next line, "The Violl once more . . . The Musick their." The music could break off when Thaisa speaks. The instrumentation that produced the rough and woeful music remains a puzzle; but the bass (gamba) viol was the member of the viol family most preferred for solo performance in Shakespeare's day. It would not be inappropriate for a violist to appear on the stage and perform the music requested by Cerimon. If so, the viol solo piece given in Figure 15 would be appropriate. This piece, "Sweete musicke," is a "lesson" for gamba viol transcribed from Tobias Hume's *Captaine Humes Poeticall Musicke* (1607).

The next performance of music occurs after Lysimachus, the governor of Mytilene, learns of Pericles' despondency and recommends the services of Marina, who he thinks might cure the King. Lysimachus remarks (V, i, 45-48), "She questionless with her sweet harmony/ And other chosen attractions, would allure,/ And make battery through his deafn'd parts,/ Which now are midway stopp'd."

Marina is brought on board Pericles' ship. She attempts to revive him with a song, as Thaisa was revived by music. Apparently she fails with the song, and it is only when she begins to relate her life story to Pericles that he begins to stir out of his coma. But we

FIGURE 15.—Sweete Musicke

may believe that the song has more importance than is apparent in the text. The Q1609(1) text indicates that Marina sings, but the song lyric is omitted. We know, however, that music was one of the notable skills of Marina, that Lysimachus believes her singing will revive Pericles, and that Marina does sing to Pericles. Why should this information be present if the song is to accomplish nothing dramatic? If we turn again to Twyne's *Painfull Adventures,* pp. 54, 55, we find a possible explanation.

In the analogous situation in Twyne's story a song is sung. Its complete lyric follows:

> Amongst the harlots foule I walke,
> yet harlot none am I:
> The Rose amongst the Thorns grows,
> and is not hurt thereby.
> The thief that stole me, sure I thinke,
> is slain before this time,
> A bawd me bought, yet I am not
> defilde by fleshly crime.
>
> ---
>
> Were nothing pleasanter to me,
> than parents mine to know:
> I am the issue of a king,
> my bloud from kings doth flow.
> I hope that God will mend my state,
> and send a better day.
> Leave off your tears, plucke up your heart,
> and banish care away.
>
> Shew gladnesse in your countenence,
> cast up your cheerfull eyes:
> That God remaines that once of nought
> created earth and skies.
> He will not let in care and thought
> you still to live, and all for nought.

It is possible that the lyric of the song is omitted in the play because Shakespeare wrote none for it, but employed Twyne's lyric, or a part of it, instead. There is a gap between the quality of Twyne's poetry and that of Shakespeare that makes us wince, yet the lyric is appropriate to the other archaisms in the play. The lyric is a little long for dramatic use; a stage version would need only the first two stanzas, those separated from the remainder with a line. It may also be noted that this scene provides one of the few instances where a song lyric is missing from a Shakespeare play. If Shakespeare used Twyne's song, or a close paraphrase of it, the following action, including the blow struck Marina by Pericles (referred to in the play but not performed) may be clarified.

Let us assume that Marina sings the opening stanzas of the song. Pericles, though outwardly comatose, dimly understands Marina's words, though he disbelieves her story. Enraged by the seeming vice in such a fair body, he pushes her away from him. As the import of her words gradually sinks in, he revives enough to question her about her story. The details are revealed, although Marina speaks as if afraid of infuriating Pericles further. The truth finally appears, and Marina and Pericles joyfully embrace.

The episode is thus a dramatic recognition accompanied by, and perhaps initiated by, music and song. Pericles is revived from a living death and brought to perceive beauty and truth in what appeared to him at first vice and falsity. Thus, the theme of the essential falsity of appearances and the discovery of a higher form of truth—the ascent of Mersenne's gamut—is marked by the sound of music.

Though the validity of the foregoing explanation may be debatable, a song is necessary here for production. In the absence of a

FIGURE 16.—Amongst the harlots foule I walke

lyric in the text, Twyne's song is an apt substitute. In Figure 16 it is given an Elizabethan musical setting—a ballad tune which fits the metrical style of the lyric. The tune was a very popular one entitled "The Spanish Pavin." The transcription is taken from J. Gibbon, *Melody and the Lyric,* p. 58.

When Pericles finally understands the import of Marina's story, he speaks:

> *Per.* I embrace you.
> Give me my robes. I am wild in my beholding.
> O heavens bless my girl! But, hark, what music?
> Tell Helicanus, my Marina, tell him
> O'er, point by point, for yet he seems to doubt,
> How sure you are my daughter. But, what music?
> *Hel.* My lord, I hear none.
> *Per.* None!
> The music of the spheres! List, my Marina.
> *Lys.* It is not good to cross him; give him way.
> *Per.* Rarest sounds! Do ye not hear?
> *Lys.* My lord, I hear.
> *Per.* Most heavenly music!

Pericles' perception of the music of the spheres, we may well believe, is both the dramatic and allegorical climax of the play. At this point Pericles has completed, both in Christian and Neo-Platonic symbolism, his pilgrim's progress. At the end of his journey he achieves sight of the Heavenly City as symbolized by the music of the spheres. Likewise, according to Mersenne, he has reached the highest notes of the cosmic gamut; he has obtained the mystic *Entendement.* It is at this point that the vision of Diana appears to him.

There is some doubt whether or not music was actually performed here. Dyce, following Malone, suggested that in Lysimachus' line in Q1609, "Musicke my lord? I heare," the word "Musicke" was actually a stage direction, and that his line should read, "My lord, I hear." *Music.*[17] Deighton followed the suggestion but remarked, "No music is mentioned in Wilkin's novel, and any music of earth would be likely to jar with that 'music of the spheres' which was already lulling Pericles to sleep."[18] Despite the dubious quality of Dyce's suggestion, it has been followed by most editors—rightfully so, if we may judge, though not for the reason advanced by Dyce. Perhaps both he and Deighton are right.

Let us suppose that the music heard by Pericles should not be heard by Marina and Lysimachus. In this event Lysimachus' line in Q1609, "Musicke my lord? I heare," would be an expression of doubt followed by agreement merely to avoid crossing the bemused Pericles. Yet even though the music is unheard by Marina and Lysimachus, it does not necessarily follow that the music should be unheard by the audience. We note that the passage just quoted contains the information—the source and purpose of the music—usually provided by Shakespeare when music is performed in the plays. Furthermore, this point of the action is a highly emotional one, the climax of the play, and we have observed Shakespeare habitually underscoring such moments with music. Finally, music here would also serve to introduce the vision of Diana; and we know that, for Shakespeare, there was a strong affinity between music and the supernatural.[19] Hence, while we might question the removal of a part of Lysimachus' Quarto line, it seems that music should be performed here whether or not a stage direction specifically calls for it.

For music in this instance, the "Measure" shown in Figure 17 might be used. This grave dance is found in the Giles Lodge Lute Book (1570); the transcription is from Mabel Dolmetsch, *Dances of England and France,* pp. 53, 54. The type of music usually associated with celestial music by the Elizabethans was played by a consort of recorders. The musicians, of course, were hidden from the audience.

FIGURE 17.—Measure

Now a word about the dumb shows. In Tudor stage practice music was almost invariably performed as an accompaniment to the dumb shows. Why, then, do we find no evidence of music being used for this purpose in *Pericles?* It may be that the practice was so ingrained that the author thought no written direction was necessary. A more likely guess is that Shakespeare called for no music with these particular dumb shows. Gower may have spoken his choruses while the dumb shows were being given, thus parts of his choruses might be running comments on the significance of the miming done on the stage. Gower explains (III, 19), "What's dumb in show I'll plain with speech." This would be one escape from the "inexplicable dumb shows" scorned by Hamlet. If so, the main function of music in such cases—to maintain a flow of sound during the pantomime—would be performed by Gower's explanations. Music would then not be necessary, especially since it might interfere with the clear projection of the information Gower offers.

To conclude, the performed music in *Pericles,* apart from what intrinsic value it may have had, seems to be used symbolically and in close association with an allegorical theme. Any excursion into symbolism, especially where Shakespeare is concerned, is risky, but an allegorical interpretation of *Pericles* in indicated by its action and characterization. And when we observe Pericles scorning sensual delights at the beginning of the play and achieving a divine vision at the end, we should be justified in assuming that there is a Christian and Platonic rationale in the play. We have discovered, also, that the philosophy of music outlined by Mersenne can be accommodated with this rationale, and that in specific instances in the play performed music is associated with crucial steps in Pericles' ascent from the world of appearances to a perception of the divine.

Notes

1. E. Chambers, *William Shakespeare,* I, 520-522; Neilson and Hill, *Complete Plays and Poems of William Shakespeare,* pp. 425, 426; Craig, *The Complete Works of Shakespeare,* pp. 1153, 1154.
2. As suggested by Chambers, *op. cit.,* pp. 520, 521. Craig believes the text is only printed (*op. cit.,* p. 1154).
3. Chambers, *op. cit.,* I, 522.

4. The basic text used in this chapter is that of Craig unless otherwise noted. This line is from the 1609(1) Quarto in the Folger Shakespeare Library. The New Cambridge edition omits "Musicke," following Malone (ed., *Works of Shakespeare,* 1790), who regularized the meter of the line.
5. Long, *Shakespeare's Use of Music,* I, 93, 107.
6. Frederick Sternfeld discusses the music of the Bower in his "*Troilus and Cressida:* Music for the Play," pp. 114, 115.
7. *Ibid.,* pp. 116-119.
8. *The patterne of Painfull Adventures,* p. 31.
9. *Ibid.,* p. 22.
10. *Ibid.,* pp. 22, 23.
11. This point is discussed more fully elsewhere. See J. Long, "Laying the Ghosts in 'Pericles,' " pp. 39-42.
12. Craig, *op. cit.,* has only the knights performing the first dance, although he inserts a stage direction calling for ladies in the second instance. His insertions are tacit.
13. T. Arbeau (*Orchesography,* p. 183) describes a masculine sword dance called the "buffens" or "matachins" in which "the dancers are dressed in small corslets, with fringe epaulets and fringe hanging from beneath their belts over a silken ground. Their helmets are made of gilded cardboard, their arms are bare and they wear bells upon their legs and carry a sword in the right hand and a shield in the left. They dance to a special tune played in duple time and accompanied by the clash of their swords and shields." This dance, while perhaps derived from a common ancestor, the classical Greek Pyrrhic dance, does not fit the description of the Knights' dance in *Pericles.*
14. Act III, iii, 106-108. This symbolism of the duet dance was common Elizabethan lore. Elyot comments in *The Gouernour,* p. 94: "It is diligently to be noted that the associatinge of man and woman in daunsing, they bothe observinge one nombre and tyme in their mevynges, was that begonne without a speciall consideration, as well for the necessarye coniunction of those two persones, as for the intimation of sondry vertues, which be by them represented. And for as moche as by the association of a man and a woman in daunsinge may be signified matrimonie, I coulde in declarynge the dignitie and commoditie of that sacrament make intiere volumes, if it were nat so communely knowen to all men. . . ."
15. See Chapter III.
16. J. Maxwell (ed., *Pericles,* new Cambridge edition, p. 154 Fn. 95) follows Malone in preferring "viall" here. He notes that both Gower and Wilkins describe liquor being poured into Thaisa's mouth. But Shakespeare does not mention the use of a liquor.
17. K. Deighton, editor of the Arden edition, p. 139. See also Mavwell, *op. cit.,* p. 190 Fn. 236, 237.
18. *Idem.*
19. Long, *Shakespeare's Use of Music,* I, 37, 39, 84, 97.

FIVE

Cymbeline

SIGNIFICANT CHANGE BECOMES APPARENT IN Shakespeare's use of music in *Cymbeline*. In keeping with the retrospective tone of the whole play, his musico-dramatic technique is that of the early comedies, though with a melodramatic emphasis foreign to his earlier practices. In one sense he turns to the past by repeating musical devices used in the early comedies; in another sense he emphasizes the capacity of music to sharpen the pathos of at least one episode. The novelty and ingenuity apparent in the use of music in the early comedies are here strengthened by a placid, yet more profound, utilization of the intrinsic and symbolic powers of the music itself; and with this new skill he enables the music to transcend its effectiveness as a clever stage device.

Such a development was perhaps natural. By 1611, the date of the first known performance of the play, Shakespeare seems to have abandoned many of the flashing conceits and other theatrical *tours de force* associated with the early plays.[1] Perhaps they were no longer appealing or necessary to a well-established dramatist secure in the favor of court and commons. Moreover, in the courtly audiences he had patrons apt to appreciate and enjoy music for its own sake as well as for its dramatic ends. The fashion of the time favored a rich musical fare; the plays of Marston, Webster, and Beaumont and Fletcher made extensive use of music, particularly as a dramatic device. When we add to these factors the great influence of the Jacobean masques on dramatic practices, it is easy to understand the interest of all the dramatists of the period in music, an interest which sometimes produced from spectators of the plays reports praising the music performed but remaining eloquently silent about the quality of the action.[2] We may feel assured that most of the dramatists of the time were aware of these factors, Shakespeare among them.

In *Cymbeline* Shakespeare apparently looked backward when he introduced the aubade offered Imogen by the scoundrelly Cloten in Act II, iii. This morning song, or hunts-up, has a counterpart in *The Two Gentlemen of Verona*—Thurio's song "Who is Sylvia?" performed under the window of the beautiful Sylvia. The music in that case, in addition to performing other functions, helped to characterize Thurio as an ineffectual lover. The same technique is used in *Cymbeline* to point up Cloten's nature—his petulance, grossness, and self-esteem—as revealed by his remarks about the music and his purpose in providing it and particularly by the obscene wordplay which introduces the music. Against this portrayal of an ugly character the fresh loveliness of one of Shakespeare's supreme lyrics stands in a dramatic contrast that must reveal a more evil Cloten than direct description could do.[3]

As the episode opens we find Cloten marshaling the musicians and courtiers in preparation for Imogen's awakening.

> *Clot.* . . . it's almost morning, is't not?
> *1.* Day, my Lord.
> *Clot.* I would this Musicke would come: I am advised to give her Musicke a mornings, they say it will penetrate.
>
> *Enter Musitians*
>
> Come on, tune: If you can penetrate her with your fingering, so: wee'l try with tongue too: if none will do, let her remaine: but Ile never give o're. First, a very excellent good conceyted thing; after a wonderful sweet aire, with admirable rich words to it, and then let her consider.
>
> SONG
>
> *Hearke, hearke, the Larke at Heavens gate sings,*
> *and Phoebus gins arise.*
> *His Steeds to water at those Springs*
> *on chalic'd Flowres that lyes:*
> *And winking Mary-buds begin to ope their Golden eyes*
> *With every thing that pretty is, my Lady sweet arise:*
> *Arise, arise.*
>
> So, get you gone: if this penetrate, I will consider your Musicke the better; if it do not, it is a voyce in her eares which Horse-haires, and Calves-guts, nor the voyce of unpaved Eunuch to boot, can never amed.[4]

The music and its immediate context thus serve to emphasize both the brutish nature of Cloten and the purity of Imogen.

The music also serves a strictly utilitarian purpose. It allows time for the actor playing the part of Imogen to make a costume change prior to his reappearance on the stage in the following scene, and it also provides time for the stage properties to be removed from the inner stage. As the scene opens, Imogen is "discovered" preparing to retire for the night. She dismisses her servants and goes to sleep; Iachimo emerges from the trunk, collects his evidence, then departs. The scene ends, evidently by the closing of the curtains in front of the inner stage. Immediately thereafter, no doubt, the boy playing the part of Imogen had to change his dress, and the stage hands began moving the bed, trunk, wall-hangings, and other properties from the inner stage. The music of Cloten's aubade would serve to fill time before Imogen's reappearance, fully dressed, and might help to cover any noise made by the stage hands in clearing the inner stage.

Cloten's remarks on the music supply a description of the manner in which the music was performed in the original performances. As in the case of the aubade in *The Two Gentlemen of Verona,* two pieces of music are played, one an instrumental "fancy" or fantasia which Cloten calls "a very excellent good conceyted thing," followed by a song, a lutenist's ayre, to judge from Cloten's description, "a wonderful sweet aire, with admirable rich words to it."[5]

Cloten and his company appear outside of Imogen's apartment, possibly in front of the curtains just previously drawn to close the bedroom scene. The musicians were doubtless three or four violists and a singer. Cloten mentions "Horse-haires," referring to a viol or violin bow, and "Calves-guts," the strings of the instruments. The instrumental fancy was usually written for a "whole" consort, a group of viols in this case. The singer was most probably a singing boy. Cloten refers to the voice as that of an "unpaved," that is, beardless, eunuch; but the Italian *castrati* were rarities in the London of 1611. The musicians join Cloten and the other lords on the outer stage, perform the fancy and the song, then leave the stage.

For the fancy the charming "Fantasy a 3" by Thomas Lupo seems fitting and practical. The complete score, as reproduced in Ernest Meyer, *English Chamber Music,* pp. 3-7, is shown in Figure 18. The original music for "Hark, hark the Lark" has yet to be recovered, but the setting found recently in the Bodleian Library by George Thewlis (see Figure 19 and the Appendix) might possibly be a version of the original.[6] This setting is anonymous and appears in Bodleian MS Don. C 57, fol. 78, which manuscript is dated about 1650. Peter Seng believes the omission of the two lines in the man-

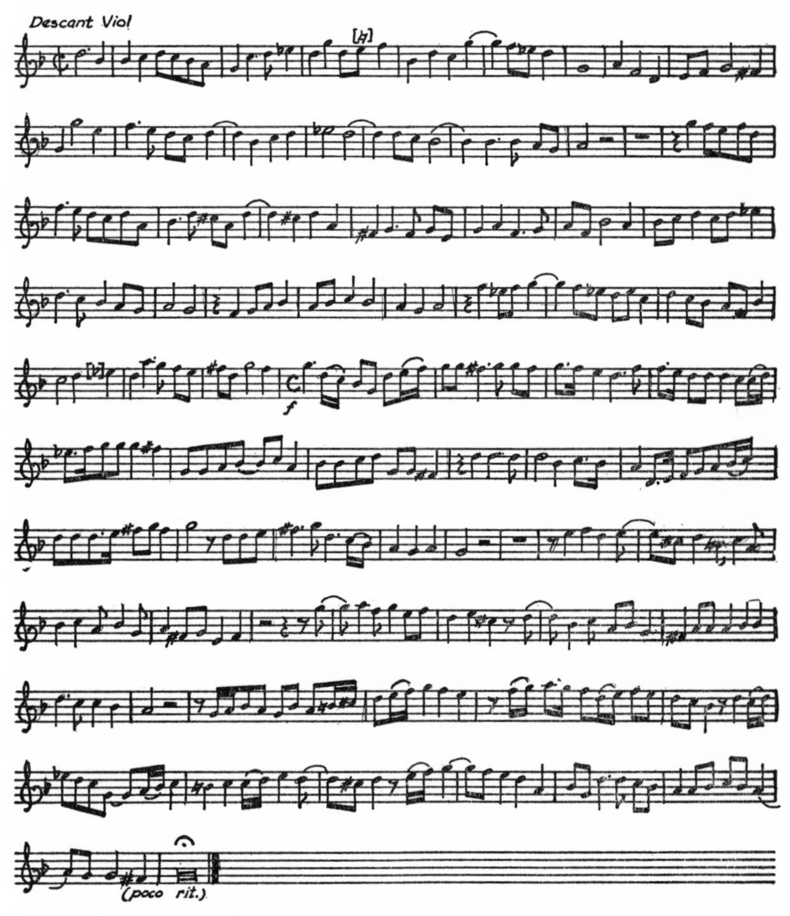

FIGURE 18a.—Fantasy a 3

uscript version is probably an abridgment to fit a melody composed after 1623: yet he also observes that the setting appears in manuscript together with music by Johnson, Wilson, and Hilton, all near contemporaries of Shakespeare.[7] All these latter composers composed music for Shakespeare's songs. Another student of the setting also notes that "the score calls for a treble voice of comparatively high range: middle F to high A," which range would agree with Cloten's description of the singer as a eunuch.[8] The use of this setting of

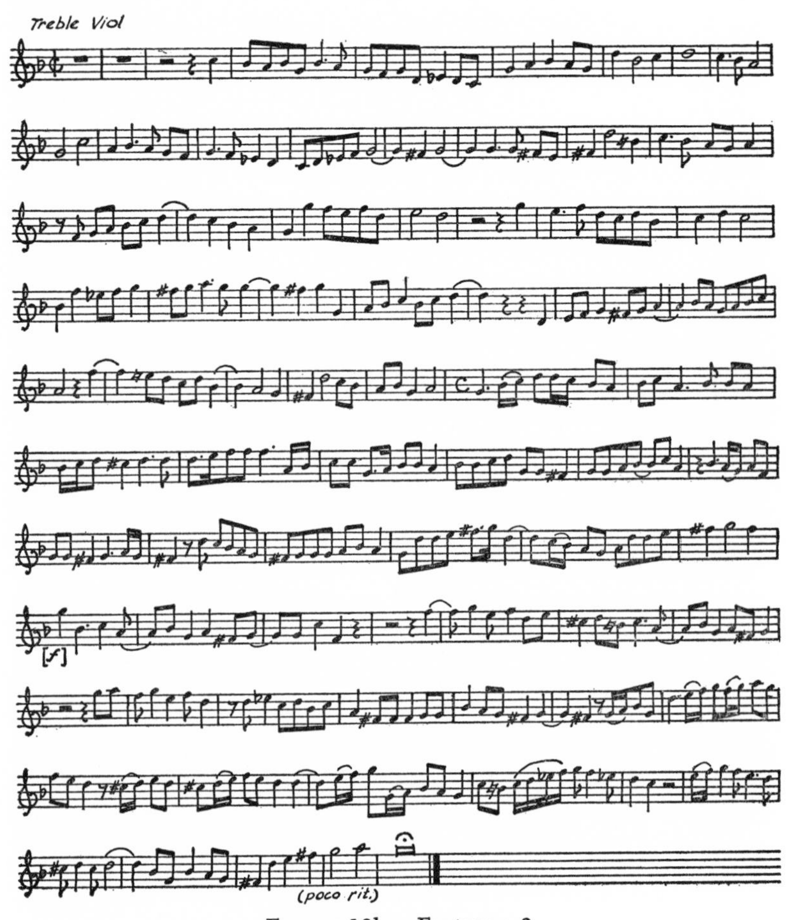

FIGURE 18b.—Fantasy a 3

"Hark, hark, the Lark" on Shakespeare's stage is hence a moot question, but the music is graceful and sophisticated; it is quite appropriate for the aubade.

The dramatic function of the music in Act IV of *Cymbeline* seems sheer melodrama. Belarius and Guiderius, meeting in the forest, are suddenly aware of solemn and mournful music sounding from the direction of the cave where they had left Imogen.

Solemn Musick

Bel. My ingenuous Instrument,
(Hearke Polidore) it sounds: but what occasion
Hath Cadwal now to give it motion? Hearke.

FIGURE 18c.—Fantasy a 3

Gui. Is he at home?
Bel. He went hence even now.
Gui. What does he meane?
Since death of my deer'st Mother
It did not speake before. All solemn things
Should answer solemne Accidents. The matter?
Triumphs for nothing, and lamenting Toyes,
Is iollity for Apes, and greefe for Boyes.
Is Cadwall mad?

Enter Aviragus, with Imogen dead, bearing her in his Armes.

There follows a lengthy passage of gentle lamentation over the supposedly dead Imogen which culminates with the familiar dirge, "Feare no more the heate o th' Sun."

As the comments of Belarius and Guiderius clearly indicate, the "Solemn Musick" serves to increase the pathos of Imogen's death; the music is aimed directly at the emotions of the audience to heighten its relish of the tender ritual which follows. The difficult

FIGURE 19.—Hark, hark, the Lark

question raised by the scene, however, appears when we seek the source of the music. Exactly what was "the ingenuous Instrument" given motion by Cadwal (Arviragus)? Shakespeare apparently suggests that the music is produced by some kind of mechanical contrivance which could play automatically in the cave. Cadwal started it and then left, bearing the body of Imogen. There is a suggestion printed in the Variorum edition (vi and viii) that the instrument referred to was an Æolian harp. A moment's reflection will raise serious doubts that this explanation holds water, or rather wind, as far as the actual performance of the music is concerned.

The Æolian harp is certainly automatic, though not "given motion," in that its music is produced by the wind—when the wind blows. Yet no prompter would depend on the vagrant wind to blow on cue, nor would the music of the Æolian harp fit the conventional Elizabethan ideas of solemn music. Of course, the use of some other mechanical device is possible: clockwork musical instruments were known at this time in London, at least as curiosities. *The Oxford Companion to Music,* p. 549, notes that in the collection of musical instruments left by Henry VIII was "a Virginal that goethe with a whele without playing uppon." It also records an account of "an organ with carillon combined, operated by keyboard, or by touching a spring, and also by the automatic action of a clock," which in 1593 Queen Elizabeth sent as a gift to the Sultan of Turkey.[9] But it would seem that if a dramatist of the period used such a device, he would have exploited its novelty to a greater extent than is apparent in this case.

The answer to this question might lie in the urge toward verisimilitude followed by the Elizabethan dramatists. We have previously observed that in the use of music on the stage the Elizabethans were rather strict observers of the convention of probability. When music was performed, a dramatist was usually careful to explain the source of the music and its dramatic functions in a way which would make the occurrence of the music probable within the play's setting and action. Sometimes, though, adherence to convention conflicted with a desire for theatrical effects. The dramatist then had to resolve the conflict as best he could.

It was this conflict of convention and special effect that might explain Shakespeare's "ingenuous Instrument." He had before him a very touching episode which could be made more pathetic by the addition of music of a solemn, mournful nature, but in the wild forests around Milford-Haven who would produce the proper music? No divine agencies were involved; therefore the music could not be plucked from the air. No audience, Shakespeare perhaps thought, would comfortably accept the sound of music without some explanation of its presence in the forest. What to do? One resolution of the dilemma could have been the invention of a mechanical instrument which, like "the music of the spheres," or "celestial music," could dispense with human musicians. The actual music was doubtless performed by musicians in the music room, screened from view of the audience.

We cannot know how successful this stratagem might have been; all things considered, it seems to the modern reader a fairly clumsy bow to the dictates of melodrama. On the Jacobean stage, however, it might have proved quite successful except to a few strict Jonsonians.

"Solemn Musick" was traditionally associated in Shakespeare's time with the music of woodwinds, most often recorders, although in the private theaters a small organ was sometimes used for sad or

FIGURE 20.—Lacrimae

solemn scenes. For a modern production an organ might well be used. A suitably mournful score would be John Dowland's "Lacrimae," one of the most popular of the composer's works at the turn of the century, and still reprinted and transcribed in modern collections of early English music. The treble viol, or cantus, part of this work, as transcribed from Morley's *First Booke of Consort Lessons* (1599), is shown in Figure 20. It is likely that the music, which begins before Arviragus appears, continued to sound, providing a lyrical background for the lamentations of Guiderius and Arviragus leading up to the singing of the dirge.

It is clear from the Folio stage direction that "Feare no more the heate o th' Sun" was intended by Shakespeare to be sung. It is also clear that in the performance of the play using the First Folio text, the dirge was not sung but spoken or declaimed. The evidence that it was spoken is in the context of the song:

Arvi. And let us (Polidore) though now our voyces
Have got the mannish cracke, sing him to 'th ground
As once to our Mother: use like note, and words,
Save that Euriphile, must be Fidele.
Guid. Cadwall,
I cannot sing: Ile weepe, and word it with thee;
For Notes of sorrow, out of tune, are worse
Then Priests, and Phanes that lye.
Arvi. Wee'l speake it then.
* * * * * * *
If you'l fetch him [Cloten's body],
Wee'l say our Song the whil'st: Brother begin.
* * * * * * *

SONG.

Guid. *Feare no more the heate o th' Sun,*
Nor the furious Winters rages,
Thou thy worldly task hast don,
Home art gon, and tane thy wages.
Golden Lads and Girles all must,
As Chimney-Sweepers come to dust.
Arvi. *Fear no more the frowne o th' Great,*
Thou art past the Tirants stroake,
Care no more to cloath and eate,

To thee the Reede is as the Oake:
The Scepter, Learning, Physicke must,
All follow this and come to dust.
Guid. *Feare no more the Lightning flash.*
Arvi. *Nor th' all-dreaded Thunderstone.*
Guid. *Feare not Slander, Censure rash,*
Arvi. *Thou hast finish'd Ioy and mone.*
Both. *All Lovers young all Lovers must,*
Consigne to thee and come to dust.
Guid. *No Exorcisor harme thee,*
Arvi. *Nor no witch-craft charme thee.*
Guid. *Ghost unlaid forbeare thee,*
Arvi. *Nothing ill come neere thee.*
Both. *Quiet consumation have,*
And renowned be thy grave.

Enter Belarius with the body of Cloten.

Gui. We have done our obsequies:
Come lay him down.

The dirge seems to accomplish two dramatic ends; it maintains and brings to a climax the emotional impact of Imogen's presumed death: and it suggests a lapse of time during which Belarius presumably seeks Cloten's body and brings it to the waiting brothers for burial.

Richmond Noble suggests that the dirge was declaimed rather than sung because the trained singers for whom it was written were not available at the performance using the Folio text. If so, this would be a strong indication that the dirge was an ayre for which music was especially written. No musical setting made for the first performances of the play is known. Therefore, in Figure 21 the song is set to a melody used by George Wither for a "Lullabie" in his

Fear no more the heat o' th' sun Nor the furious Winter's rages.
Thou thy worldly task hast done Home art gone, and ta'en thy wages.
Golden Lads, and Girls all must, As Chimney - Sweepers come to dust.

FIGURE 21.—Feare no more the heate o th' Sun

hymn collection *Haleluiah* (1641). Before Wither used it, the tune was popular as a setting for a paternoster attributed to Martin Luther.[10]

The masque scene in *Cymbeline* (V, iv) has been considered an extraneous interpolation which disturbs the unity of the play.[11] This opinion has little to recommend it if the symbolic function of the music and dance be considered. Following a pattern established much earlier, for example in *A Midsummer Night's Dream,* Shakespeare places the masque and its music just before the resolution of the dramatic conflict in *Cymbeline.* In the earlier play the resolution of the difficulties enmeshing the mortals is preceded by the reestablishment of harmonious relationships in the fairy world, as symbolized by a duet dance performed by Oberon and Titania. In *Cymbeline,* likewise, the strands of the action are almost hopelessly tangled until Posthumus' parents and brothers appear to him in a dream, intercede for him by calling to Jupiter, and receive the god's assurance that all will turn out for the best. This is of course a modification of the old *deus ex machina,* but the ending of the play is not structurally dependent upon it since the seeds of the resolution were planted early in the play. Rather, the function of the masque seems purely symbolic of the death, resurrection, reunion, and reconciliation theme pervading the final comedies.

Posthumus, thought a Roman by the victorious Britons, has been imprisoned and sentenced to die. Believing that his wife is unchaste and that he has taken her life, he is content to die since he equates death with spiritual freedom. Unlike Othello, he places his fate wholly in the hands of the gods. When left alone in prison, he soliloquizes:

Post. Most welcome, bondage; for thou art a way,
(I thinke) to liberty: yet am I better
Then one that's sicke o'th'Gowt, since he had rather
Groane so in perpetuity, then be cur'd
By 'th' sure Physitian, Death: who is the key
T'unbarre these Lockes. My Conscience, thou art fetter'd
More then my shanks, & wrists: you good Gods give me
The penitent Instrument to picke that Bolt,
Then free for ever . . .

> For Imogens deere life, take mine, and though
> 'Tis not so deere, yet 'tis a life; you coyn'd it . . .
> Oh Imogen, Ile speake to thee in silence.

Solemne Musicke. Enter (as in an Apparation) Sicillius Leonatus, Father to Posthumus, an old man, attyred like a warriour, leading in his hand an ancient Matron (his wife, & Mother to Posthumus) with Musicke before them. Then: after other Musicke followes the two young Leonati (Brothers to Posthumus) with wounds as they died in the warrs. They circle Posthumus round as he lies sleeping.

As in *Pericles* the gods are merciful, and in the scene immediately following the masque Posthumus is reunited with Imogen, Cymbeline with his two sons, Belarius and Iachimo are forgiven, the evil Queen dies, and the play ends on a chord of tranquil reconciliation and universal love. Here again, as in *Pericles,* music accompanies the "voice from the whirlwind" which brings the mystic tranquillity to the troubled mortals of the play.

FIGURE 22.—Pavane

It is difficult for us to realize the impact of the vision scene on an audience, since we must work from a reading version of the comedy; yet the masque must have been very impressive. The same elements observed in the duet dance of Oberon and Titania—the supernatural, music, and the dance—are present here, though more formal and solemn. Regarding the performance of the music, the stage directions are ambiguous: either the parents are preceded on the stage by musicians, and the brothers by other musicians, or each couple is preceded by a strain of music. Probably the latter choice is correct, for the musicians were usually hidden when they produced music assigned to a supernatural origin.

We may then imagine the vision as being performed in this manner: As Posthumus concludes his soliloquy and throws himself down on the floor of his cell, the air is almost imperceptibly stirred by the sound of soft and solemn music which grows louder as Posthumus gradually sinks into a profound sleep. At the end of this first strain of music, the hidden musicians (probably a consort of recorders) sound another strain to which the figures of Sicillius Leonatus and his wife appear. Moving gravely yet gracefully in time with the music, they approach Posthumus and stand above his head. The music changes to another strain, whereupon the young Leonati ap-

FIGURE 23.—Pavane

pear, moving in the same sober gait as the parents. They take their position at the foot of the sleeper. Then, as the music continues, the spectres circle Posthumus in a formalized dance, at the conclusion of which the music ceases and the lines of the masque are intoned by the figures. This is the final performance of music in the play, although a kettledrum sounds the thunder which accompanies Jupiter's descent and ascent on the stage lift.

The musical scores for this scene, if it were performed as reconstructed, would probably have consisted of three of the statelier dance forms, perhaps pavanes. In Figures 22, 23, and 24 appear three pavanes by Holborne, taken from his *Pavans, galliards, almains, and other short aeirs . . .* (1599).

Other than the stilted poetry in the masque, which may have been purposely written so to suit the masque form and the particular situation, there is little reason for believing the scene to be a spectacular theatrical interpolation. The increasing use of the masque devices in Shakespeare's later plays could well be a natural development, a logical adaptation of his play-within-the-play device to the sophisticated, courtly, masque-loving audiences before whom the King's Men regularly performed and to whom they owed much of their prosperity.

FIGURE 24.—Pavane

Notes

1. E. Chambers, *William Shakespeare,* I, 485.
2. Gamaliel Ratsey, in *Ratseis Ghost,* p. 4, addresses a group of players: "I pray you (quoth Ratsey) let me heare your musicke, for I have often gone to plaies more for musicke sake, then for action."
3. H. Furness (Variorum edition, p. 127 Fn.) notes the contrast.
4. All quotations from the play are taken from the First Folio.
5. As E. Naylor notes, *Shakespeare and Music,* p. 71.
6. The transcription in Figure 19 is by G. A. Thewlis. For further discussions of this setting see his "Some Notes on a Bodleian Manuscript," pp. 32-35; Willa Evans, "Shakespeare's 'Harke, Harke, ye Larke,'" pp. 98-103; and Peter Seng, *The Dramatic Function of the Songs . . . ,* pp. 550-557.
7. *Op. cit.,* pp. 556, 557.
8. Evans, *op. cit.,* p. 99.
9. An entry in the Coventry Chamberlains' Accounts for November, 1624, notes: "Rewards to king's and prince's trumpeters, Lady Elizabeth's players. Given to Bartholomew Cloys being allowed by the master of the Revels for showing a musical organ with divers strange and rare motions, 5s." See W. Woodfill, *Musicians in English Society,* p. 285. Leonardo da Vinci devised several automatic musical instruments, but none of them is known to have been constructed. Among them were a mechanical viol and a "viola organista," rather like an organistrum or hurdy-gurdy, operated by a clockwork mechanism. He also designed an organ which would automatically play a four-part canon. Sketches of these instruments may be seen in the Elmer Belt Library of Vinciana, Los Angeles, MSS H. 45v, B. 50v, and B.M. 137v.
10. J. Gibbon, *Melody and the Lyric,* p. 163.
11. According to Chambers, *op. cit.,* I, 486, and Furness, *op. cit.,* pp. vii, viii.

SIX

The Winter's Tale

ONSIDERED FROM THE POINT OF VIEW OF DRAmatic unity and probability, *The Winter's Tale* is not a good play. This critical commonplace is stated again because it is a common observation. Yet this view, while true as far as it goes, need not obscure the fact that the play was quite popular at its early performances. Apparently, within the limits which Shakespeare set for the play, it was successful in the eyes of the audience for which he wrote, which implies that it contained those elements most likely to please that audience. Music, of course, played its part in making the play a success. It would be well, then, to determine as far as possible what the author intended for his play to achieve, and then to observe the functions of the music in helping to make that achievement possible.

Thomas Marc Parrott has given, in general, one objective description of the play's purpose. "One does not look," he remarks, "for real life realistically presented in such plays [tragicomedies], but for lively action abounding in surprise and sensation, and there is plenty of this in *The Winter's Tale*. . . . Surprise, sensation, and spectacle are for the spectator of this rarely presented play. . . .[1] If we accept this comment on the play, then we may say that the over-all purpose of the music is to contribute to the surprise, sensation, and spectacle of the comedy.

The manner in which the music performs this comprehensive function is closely related not only to the play itself but also to the audience for which the drama was written and to certain circumstances connected with the early productions, particularly the popularity of the Jacobean masques. We have observed, out of the corner of our eyes, the influence of the masque form on *Love's Labour's Lost, A Midsummer Night's Dream,* and *The Merry Wives of Windsor.*[2] This influence becomes pervasive in the final comedies, notably in *Pericles* and *Cymbeline,* is clearly apparent in *The Winter's Tale,* and finally produces, in *The Tempest,* a dramatic form which may best be described by the term "masque-drama." The time has come, therefore, to examine more closely the Jacobean masque and its impact on the two final comedies of Shakespeare. At present, however, we shall be concerned primarily with the music in *The Winter's Tale.*

To begin, let us take a quick sample of the dramatic atmosphere in which Shakespeare found himself when he wrote the play about 1610. He was a shareholder, with Robert Armin and others, in the King's Men, a well-established and popular dramatic company charged with the presentation of plays at the Court as well as in the company's two playhouses, the Globe and Blackfriars. We may safely assume that as a responsible member of his company Shakespeare would write the kind of play that would appeal to both court and commons, that is, a popular play containing some characteristics of the court masque.

The period roughly from 1607 to 1635 witnessed the full flowering of the Jacobean masque in all its extravagant glory. This brilliant era was ushered in by the construction in 1607-1608 of a new, permanent banqueting house at Whitehall especially designed for the staging of masques.[3] A succession of brilliant productions followed, including the *Masque of Queens* (1608-1609), *Love Freed from Ignorance and Folly* (1610-1611), *Oberon* (1611), and *Love Restored* (1612), by Jonson; *Tethy's Festival* (1610); by Daniels; *The Masque for Lord Hayes* (1607), *The Earl of Somerset's Masque* (1612), *The Lord's Masque* (1613), by Campion; *The Masque of the Middle Temple and Lincoln's Inn* (1613), by Chapman; and Beaumont's *Masque of the Inner Temple and Gray's Inn* (1613).[4] The latter three were given as parts of the celebration of the marriage of Princess Elizabeth to the Elector Palatine, Frederick V, on February 14, 1613.[5] In several of these masques Queen Anne was a participant.[6] The year 1613 seems to have been the climax of the masque as an amusement popular with the Court. With the death of Anne in 1619 the masque, at least in its spectacular and extravagant forms, was well on the way to oblivion.

When Shakespeare wrote *The Winter's Tale,* he was therefore in the midst of an audience which delighted in the fantasy, the artificiality, the allegorical-pastoral-classical themes, the music, dance, spectacle, and declamation, all found in the Stuart masques. This fairyland world is described by Allardyce Nicoll in *Stuart Masques and the Renaissance Stage,* pp. 192, 201:

> Into this strange array of allegorical figures [Bacchus, Comus, Silenus, Satyrs, etc.] come, bravely clad or in rags, a motley crowd of persons, ancient and modern, highborn and low, from Western lands and from the Orient. . . . The underworld of seventeenth-century England spawns here—Knaves and Ruffians, Thieves, Tinkers, Beggars, Coiners, Bawds, Midwives, and Courtesans, Mountebanks, Jugglers, Ballad-singers, Fiddlers, Mock-musicians, and Morescoes. A Bearward leads forward his performing animal; a Pedlar sells his wares; while a Seller of Tinderboxes and a Crier of Mousetraps announce their goods.

There can be little doubt that Shakespeare was in the midst of this fantastic world or that he saw in it an almost inexhaustible mine for his own uses. Certainly his fellow dramatists were quick to incorporate as much of the masque flavor into their plays as they could.[7]

The influence of the masque on *The Winter's Tale* may perhaps account for the presence of the bear on the stage (III, iii), and for the resurrection scene (V). Transformations were stock devices in the masques. In Jonson's *Oberon,* Oberon appears in a chariot drawn by two white bears. The transformation of statues into men or women is an effect used in many masques; Campion's *Lords Masque* shows eight statues changed into women, and in his *Earl of Somerset's Masque* twelve knights are brought to life after having been changed by enchantment into golden pillars.[8] Shakespeare need not have harked back to Marston's *Pygmalion's Image;* statues were coming to life all around him as he wrote the final comedies.

The effects of the masques on the entire play is a study beyond the scope of this chapter, though one which deserves more attention than has been given it. What we may consider, however, is the relationship between the masques and the music in the play. This kinship seems to be a close one, for much of the fourth act is apparently constructed as a masque within the play. If we reduce the various theatrical sections of the masques to a typical skeleton, do the same for the fourth act of the play, then compare the two, the resemblance can easily be seen.

The Stuart masques varied widely in details of theme, spectacle, and costume, but the arrangement of the elements, including music, dialogue or declamation, and dance, fell into a well-defined pattern. As traced by Otto Gombosi,[9] the typical masque pattern opened with a spoken or sung presentation or invocation, sometimes in the form of an incantation or transfiguration. After this the noblemen-maskers entered the "dancing place" and danced their Entry or First Dance, then followed an optional number of speeches, after which the Second, or Main Dance was performed. The Revels then began, wherein the maskers chose ladies from among the courtly spectators and danced with them a series of light dances starting with a measure, or pavane, and continuing with galliards, corantos, and voltas. Then a Resting Song was performed by professional singers, usually followed by the Departing Dance of maskers. A Goodnight Song or speech concluded the masque. The anti-masque—the grotesque or fantastic dances presented by professionals — sometimes preceded, sometimes followed, the Revels.

Shakespeare could not hope to reproduce this complete pattern with the means at his disposal, but he could produce an abstract that would imitate closely the masque structure. That the musical portion of the fourth act of *The Winter's Tale* does follow this pattern can be seen in the following comparison of Campion's *Masque for Lord Hayes* and of Jonson's *Oberon* with the festival portion of Shakespeare's play.

Masque for Lord Hayes[10]	*Oberon*[11]	*The Winter's Tale*
Song	Declamation	Song "When Daffodils begin to peere"
Declamation	Satyr's song	Monologue
Dialogue song	Declamation	Song "But shall I go mourne for that, my deere?"
Declamation	Song	Dialogue

Masque for Lord Hayes	*Oberon*	*The Winter's Tale*
Dance song	Satyr's dance	Song "Jog-On"
Declamation	Declamation	Dialogue
Transformation song	Song	Shepherd's dance
Declamation	Song	Dialogue
Choral song	Declamation	Song "Lawn as white as driven snow"
Dance	Duet song	Dialogue
Declamation	Fays' dance	Song "Get you hence"
Motet	Choral song	Dialogue
Dance	First maskers' dance	Song "Will you buy any Tape?"
Declamation	Song	Dialogue
Dialogue song	Maskers' dance	Satyrs' dance
Declamation	Duet song	Dialogue concluding Act IV
Light Dance (Revels)	Light dances (Revels)	
Declamation	Song	
Dance	Declamation	
Dialogue song	Maskers' dance	
Choral closing song	Closing song	

As can be seen, the music, dance, and speech sections of the three are similar and are placed in a similar sequence. Of course, in the masques where music and dance are the dominant features, the spoken portions are relatively short. Contrariwise, in the play where the dialogue dominates, the music and dance sections are relatively brief. The impress of the masque form on the sheepshearing festival seems evident.

The distinctive fact about the music in this play is that all of it, except the music played to revive Hermione in Act V, is placed in two closely related scenes. Moreover, as already shown, the music is arranged in a pattern which conforms closely to that of the great masques being produced at the time the play was written. We may therefore tentatively assume that the over-all purpose of the music is to supply one of the masque elements which delighted Shakespeare's original audiences. But a good dramatic craftsman is not usually satisfied to achieve only one effect with a particular dramatic device if the device can be made to serve other purposes. A closer look at the individual musical episodes in the play will reveal several other reasons why Shakespeare may have employed the music as he did.

The obvious use of the initial music, which Shakespeare withheld until Act IV, is to change the character of the play from the tragic to the comic. Gone now is the winter of Leontes' discontent, and spring is over the countryside. The earliest flowers are opening, the farmers' linens are hung over the hedgerows to dry in the warm sunlight. Strolling along a rustic lane, carolling lustily out of sheer high spirits, is Autolycus, that exuberant rogue who is out to pick up any dishonest penny he can from the sleepily stirring countryfolk.

ACT IV
Scena Tertia
Enter Autolicus singing.

When Daffadils begin to peere,
With heigh ho the Doxy over the dale,
Why then comes in the sweet o'the yeere,
For the red blood raigns in ye winters pale.

The white sheets bleaching on the hedge,
With hey the sweet birds, O how they sing:
Doth set my pugging tooth on edge,
For a quart of Ale is a dish for a King.

The Larke that tirra Lyra chaunts,
With heigh, the Thrush and the Iay:
Are Summer songs for me and my Aunts,
While we lye tumbling in the hay.[12]

As a part of its use to change the mood, the song contributes to the setting and characterization of the play. The scene shifts from the palace of Polixenes to the countryside, and the new setting is established by Autolycus, who paints a musical backdrop of spring flowers, hedgerows, and convenient haymows. At the same time he reveals himself as a rascal, but also a sympathetic rascal. That such a character can immediately enlist the sympathy of the spectator is due, in large measure, to the fact that he is singing a lilting song. The association of attractive characters with song was a convention well established in Shakespeare's time. As William Bowden notes in

The English Dramatic Lyric . . ., p. 44, "When a gang of thieves or gypsies or beggars first break into song, one knows immediately that they are Gilbert and Sullivan rogues, not scoundrels. . . . Song is, of course, only one means of distinguishing sympathetic characters, but it is a reliable and a popular one."

The song is a picaresque ballad filled with underworld cant. It was sung, very likely, to a rather simple ballad tune. Figure 25 shows it set to a tune entitled "Row well, ye mariners," which was entered in the Stationers' Register in 1565-1566 and was published in Thomas Robinson's *Schoole of Music* (1603).[13]

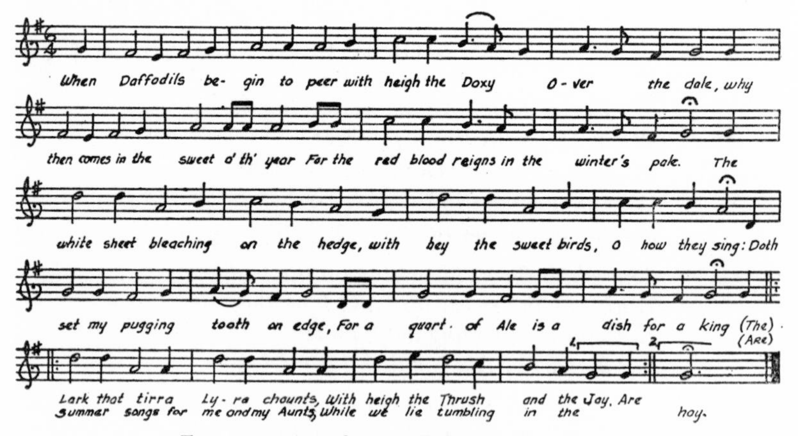

FIGURE 25.—When Daffadils begin to peere

After the performance of three stanzas Autolycus stops singing long enough to inform us that he is a former servant of Prince Florizel. He then resumes singing with what Collier believed to be two separate songs sung to differing tunes.[14]

But shall I go mourne for that (my deere)
the pale Moone shines by night
And when I wander here, and there
I then do most go right.

If Tinkers may have leave to live,
and beare the Sow-skin Bowget,
Then my account I well may give
and in the Stockes avouch-it.

While it is possible that these two stanzas are extracts from different songs, their metrical and structural patterns are so similar that they may easily be sung to the same tune. They have been set, therefore, to an old tune, "The Noble Shirve," believed to be of or before the reign of James I. The tune appears in Chappell's *Old English Popular Music,* I, 126 (see Fig. 26).

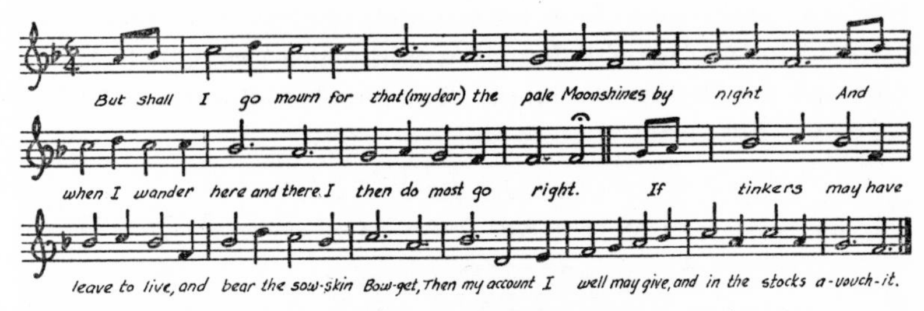

FIGURE 26.—But shall I go mourne for that (my deere)
If Tinkers may have leave to live

As the daffodil song serves as an "entering song" for Autolycus, so the merry rogue strolls off the stage happily singing another song of the open road:

Iog-on, Iog-on the foot path way,
And merrily hent the Stile-a:
A merry heart goes all the day.
Your sad tyres in a Mile-a. *Exit.*

This is a portion of a song that retained its popularity for a long time. The music to which it was probably sung appears in the Fitzwilliam Virginal Book (1603?-1612?) under the name "Hanskin." Settings of the song also appear in J. Playford's *The English Dancing Master* (1630-1698) under the title "Jog-on," and in *The Antidote against Melancholy* (1661) with an additional stanza:

Cast care away, let sorrow cease,
A fig for melancholy;
Let's laugh and sing, or, if you please,
We'll frolic with sweet Dolly.

John Hilton made the setting of the song, printed in Playford's *Catch that Catch Can* (1667), p. 85, which is shown in Figure 27 and the Appendix. It has long been known to scholars and has been published several times in modern studies, for example, in Naylor's *Shakespeare and Music,* p. 185.

The next scene presents the sheepshearing festival with full Arcadian flavor. Bucolic lads and lasses, wildly gamboling satyrs, the strains of bagpipes, pipe, and tabor, all form the background for the fresh, idyllic love of Florizel and Perdita. But this background contains somber colors both created and, ironically, accented by its music. The shadow of Polixenes' wrath, which gradually envelopes the festival, is fed by the music. This parallel movement of music

Jog on, Jog on the Foot-path way, and merrily hent the Stile-a, the Merry heart goes
all day long, the Sad tyres in a Mile-a: Your palt-ry Money Bags of Gold, what
need have we to stare ------- for, when little or nothing soon is told, and we have the lass -------
to care for: Cast care away, care away, let sorrow cease, a fig for Melan - cho - ly, let's
laugh and sing, laugh and sing, or if you please, we'll frolick with sweet Mol - ly Jog on, etc.

FIGURE 27.—Iog-on, Iog-on the foot path way

and action in the scene is made possible, apparently, by the use of pantomime while the music is being performed and by the particular songs and dances involved.

This interesting technique not only unifies the music performed, but also clarifies and enriches the characterization of Polixenes, who apparently is assigned most of the pantomime. We first become aware that Polixenes occupies a larger place in the scene than the number of spoken lines given him would indicate when the Clown calls attention to what has been happening on the stage while the dialogue song is sung by Autolycus, Mopsa, and Dorcas. In fact, he apparently cuts the song short, saying, "Wee'l have this song out anon by our selves: My Father and the Gent. are in sad talke, & wee'll not trouble them. . . ." The pantomimed "sad talke" is done, of course, by Polixenes and the old Shepherd, who begin their "conversation" as the dance of shepherds and shepherdesses ends. The combination of music and pantomime produces an ironic little drama which, if considered a modification of Shakespeare's "play-within-the-play" device, might rival Hamlet's Mousetrap in effective construction.

The growing anger of Polixenes, in opposition to the revelry of the scene, supplies the conflict of the little drama, and of course the romantic union of Florizel and Perdita is partially the cause of the revelry. Under the festive sea moves a turgid undertow of anger actually nourished by the revelry, hence the irony of the episode. Just before the shepherds' dance, Polixenes refers to Perdita as ". . . the prettiest Low borne Lasse that ever/ Ran on the greene-sord: Nothing she do's or seemes/ But smackes of something greater then her selfe,/ Too Noble for this place." And yet as he cruelly, if self-righteously, breaks off the engagement of Florizel and Perdita, he can exclaim at her as he stalks away from the shattered revels:

> And you Enchantment. . . .
> If ever henceforth, thou
> These rurall Latches, to his entrance open,
> Or hope his body more, with thy embraces,
> I will devise a death, as cruell for thee
> As thou art tender to't.

Polixenes is no Leontes subject to unreasonable outbursts of temper; and certainly Perdita has done or said nothing to attract his anger so violently toward her, unless the refusal of Florizel to seek permission of his father to marry her could cause Polixenes to seek an indirect object of his fury. How did this change occur? If we may observe the thoughts of Polixenes as the songs and dances are performed, we may see that his thoughts seem to grow out of each piece of music, and that very likely he signals these thoughts by means of pantomime to the audience while the merrymaking is in progress. Then, when he does speak at the conclusion of the Satyrs' Dance, he announces in an aside his decision to separate the two lovers, then recapitulates the reasons leading to the decision. As we shall observe, his "reasoning" forms a distorted analogy to the songs and dances in both subject and sequence.

Heere a Daunce of Shepheards and Shepheardesses. As he watches Florizel and Perdita dancing together, Polixenes sees their mutual interest only as light dalliance between a prince and an unusually attractive girl. "Sooth, when I was yong,/ and handed love as you do. . . ." And when Autolycus sings his first peddler's cry, Polixenes is strengthened in his belief that Florizel is, as the actual rustics seem to be, interested in a light love that can be purchased with trinkets.

Enter Autolycus singing.

Lawne as white as driven Snow,
Cypresse blacke as ere was Crow,
Gloves as sweete as Damaske Roses,
Maskes for faces, and for noses:
Bugle-bracelet, Necke-lace Amber,
Perfume for a Ladies Chamber:
Golden Quoifes, and Stomachers
For my Lads, to give their deers:
Pins, and poaking-stickes of steele.
What Maids lacke from head to heele:
Come buy of me, come: come buy, come buy,
Buy Lads, or else your Lasses cry: Come buy.

"I was wont/ To load my Shee with knackes: I would have ransackt/ The Pedlers silken Treasury, and have powr'd it/ To her acceptance." Polixenes naturally expects Florizel to buy Perdita a trifle from the peddler. When the Prince does not buy, the worldly father, as he listens to the dialogue song of Autolycus, Mopsa, and Dorcas, concludes that the next step will be a display of pretty pouting by Perdita in the course of which she will accuse Florizel of not loving her, accuse him of having another, secret love.

Song *Get you hence for I must goe*
Aut. *Where it fits not you to know.*
Dor. *Whether?*
Mop. *O whether?*
Dor. *Whether?*
Mop. *It becomes thy oath full well,*
Thou to me thy secrets tell.
Dor. *Me too: Le me go thether:*
Mop *Or thou goest to th' Grange, or Mill,*

Dor: *If to either thou dost ill,*
Aut: *Neither.*
Dor: *What neither?*
Aut: *Neither.*
Dor: *Thou hast sworne my Love to be,*
Mop *Thou hast sworne it more to mee.*
Then whether goest? Say whether?

Now Polixenes expects Florizel to give in to the petulance of the mercenary little wench. He is therefore somewhat startled when he notes that Autolycus picks up his pack and strolls away without selling to Florizel.

Song. *Will you buy any Tape, or Lace for your Crpe?*
My dainty Ducke, my deere-a?
Any Silke, any Thred, any Toyes for your head
Of the news't, and Fins't, fins't weare-a.
Come to the Pedler, Money's a medler,
That doth utter all mens ware-a. *Exit*

Hardly has Autolycus departed when the Satyrs perform their wild leaps and bounds "to rough for some." *Heere a Dance of twelve Satyres.*

As he observes these hairy beast-men, time out of mind the symbols of unbridled lust and carnality, Polixenes is struck by another thought. The interest of Perdita in Florizel is more than mercenary; she desires his body as well as his money. This is more serious, for physical lust cannot be bought off with a few knacks. Now Perdita becomes in his mind a seductress with stark sexual cravings as her motivation and Prince Florizel as her victim.

When Florizel offers to contract marriage with Perdita, Polixenes recalls with horror the advice he earlier had given to Perdita:

. . . you see (sweet Maid) we marry
A gentler Sien, to the wildest Stocke,
And make Conceyve a barke of baser kinde
By bud of Nobler race. This is an Art
Which do's mend Nature: change it rather, but
The Art it selfe, is Nature.
* * * * * * *

Then make you Garden rich in Gilly'vors,
And do not call them bastards.

To which Perdita had replied:

> Ile not put
> The Dible in earth, to set one slip of them:
> No more than were I painted, I would wish
> This youth should say 'twer well: and only therefore
> Desire to breed by me.

Fair is foul, and foul is fair! What witchcraft hovers through the festive air? Perdita, the "Queene of Curds and Creame," has become a vampire sucking the blood of the state. Well might Polixenes turn savagely on her:

> And thou, fresh peece
> Of excellent Witchcraft, whom of force must know
> The royall Foole thou coap'st with.
> . . . you Enchantment
> . . . If ever henceforth, thou
> These rurall Latches, to his entrance open,
> Or hope his body more, with thy embraces,
> I will devise a death, as cruell for thee
> As thou are tender to't.

At its climax, the exchange of vows between Florizel and Perdita, the little festival-tragedy ends. Perdita speaks the epilogue: "This dreame of mine/ Being now awake, Ile Queene it no inch farther,/ But milke my Ewes, and weepe."

The part played by the music in the structure of this play-within-the-play seems clear and impressive in its cumulative effect. In considering the musical episodes as an esthetic group, however, we should not overlook other dramatic functions performed by each musical incident. Let us turn back to the beginning of the sheep-shearing festival.

Prince Florizel and Perdita, the milkmaid-princess, are the Cinderella and Prince Charming of this occasion. They are the King and Queen of the festival, and the shepherds' dance symbolizes their union. Florizel tells us this when, taking Perdita's hand, he invites her to dance, saying, "But come, our dance I pray,/ Your hand (my Perdita:) so Turtles paire/ That never meane to part. . . .*Heere a Daunce of Shepheards and Shepheardesses.*" This use of a dance to symbolize the union of lovers, as we have noted, appears in several of Shakespeare's plays. And, of course, what pastoral scene would be complete without a shepherds' dance?

The dance is a group dance, perhaps a roundel. A rustic "hay" would be appropriate. The bagpipe and pipe and tabor mentioned by the servant shortly after the dance is completed would have provided fitting music. In Figure 28 is shown a hay taken from Arbeau's *Orchesography* (1589), p. 170.

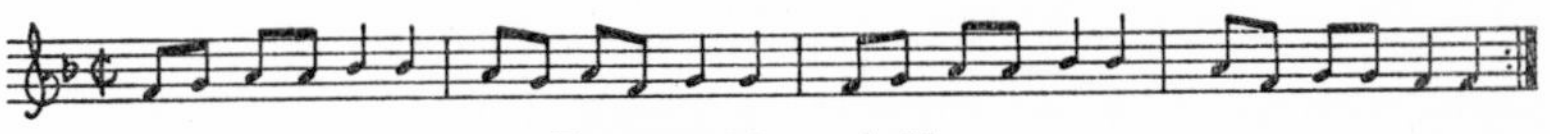

FIGURE 28.— A Hay

Hardly is the dance completed when a servant enters, reporting at length and in glowing terms the vocal prowess of a strange peddler.

> O Master: if you did but heare the Pedlar at the doore, you would never dance againe after a Tabor and Pipe: no, the Bagpipe could not move you: hee singes severall Tunes, faster then you'l tell money: he utters them as he had eaten ballads and all mens eares grew to his Tunes.

After more encomiums in a like vein, in strolls our old acquaintance, Autolycus, now in the guise of a ballad-singing peddler lustily crying his wares, "Lawne as white as driven Snow."

If we may judge by John Wilson's setting of this song in his *Cheerful Ayres or Ballads* (1660), its intrinsic value was considerable (see Fig. 29 and the Appendix). Although Wilson, in age, was not a contemporary of Shakespeare, he provides the earliest known setting of the song. A Levytype of Wilson's setting is printed in the Variorum edition, pp. 388, 389.

As a part of the festive scene we would expect ballad-singers to frequent such a convivial gathering. And since this particular peddler is Autolycus, we might also expect some knavery before the scene closes. As Bowden remarks (*op. cit.*, p. 68), "There is a well-established tradition that thieves and pickpockets shall sing to distract or to disarm their intended victims." Perhaps this is true in this case. Following the song, the Clown complains that he can buy nothing because he had earlier been cozened of his money (by Autolycus, of course). To this Autolycus, apparently the soul of probity, replies, "And indeed Sir, there are Cozeners abroad, therefore it behooves men to be wary." It is not long before Autolycus busies himself in picking the pockets of the unwary rustics.

Almost immediately after his entrance song Autolycus demon-

FIGURE 29.— Lawne as white as driven Snow

strates his skill at part-singing by performing a dialogue song with Mopsa and Dorcas.

> *Aut.* This is a merry ballad, but a very pretty one.
> *Mop.* Let's have some merry ones.
> *Aut.* Why this is a passing merry one, and goes to the tune of two maids wooing a man: there's scarse a Maide westward but she sings it: if thou'lt beare a part, thou shalt heare, tis in three parts.
> *Dor:* We had the tune on't, a month agoe.
> *Aut:* I can beare my part, you must know 'tis my occupation: Have at it with you:
> *Song Get you hence, for I must goe*

Two early musical settings of the dialogue song exist in the Drexel Collection of the Music Division of the New York Public Library. Both were recently published for the first time by John Cutts.[15] The complete setting, Figure 30 and the Appendix, appears in Drexel MS 4175 as song 59 (c. 1620).[16] This manuscript was the property of Stafford Smith, author of *Musica Antiqua* (1812), from whom it passed into the library of Edward Francis Rimbault, and from thence to the Drexel Collection. Cutts believes the song may have been composed by Robert Johnson. He states:

> Probably the music was composed by Robert Johnson: the manuscript, although it presents no attribution to him, gives it in close proximity to several compositions certainly or almost certainly by him —"Come away Hecket" from Middleton's *The Witch,* c. 1610, "Deare doe not your faire bewty wronge" from May's *The Old Couple,* c. 1615, "O let us howle" (XLII) from Webster's *The Duchesse of Malfy,* 1613, "Tell me dearest what is love" from Beaumont and Fletcher's *The Captaine,* c. 1611, and "Have you seene the bright lilly growe" (XLIX) from Jonson's *The Divell is an Asse,* 1616. The fact that all these plays were produced by the King's Men, for whom Robert Johnson was busily writing in the theater and at court between 1608 and 1617, makes it not inconceivable that the setting is Robert Johnson's.[17]

The melody is written in the treble clef throughout with an

accompaniment in lute tablature. The music obviously was written to fit the text. It seems to be an ayre written by a literate composer in imitation of a folk song.

The fragmentary setting, also anonymous, is in Drexel MS 4041.[18] This setting seems to have been made considerably later than the first discussed; it is found among song settings of sonnets by Suckling and Denham. The manuscript is probably a Restoration collection. Although the music is fragmentary, enough of it was recorded to be quite informative. The melody is the same as that of the first setting, though transposed to another key. But the second setting lacks some of the ornamentation of the first. The second is also written with a bass "continuo," or bass (gamba) viol accompaniment, instead of the lute tablature of the first. Perhaps of most interest, the vocal parts of this version are divided into treble clef for

FIGURE 30.—Get you hence, for I must goe

the two feminine parts and bass clef for the masculine part. The parts assigned in Figure 30 are according to this manuscript.

While the music of the version in Drexel MS 4041 is incomplete, the text of the song appears in full, with the addition of a second stanza. The text of the first stanza differs only slightly from that of the First Folio. The second stanza text follows:

> never more for lasses sake
> Will I danse at fare or wake
> Ah mee
> O ah mee
> Ah mee
> who shall then were a racee [?] shooe
> or what shall ye bagpipe doe
> recant or else you slay mee

recant or else you slay mee:
if thou leave our Andorne [?] greene
where shall fill or fritz [?] be seene
sleeping
what sleeping
sleeping
no Ile warrant thee, sitting sadly
or idely walking madly
in some darke, in some darke, darke Corner weeping
in some darke, darke Corner weeping.

This stanza contains one more line than the first stanza, "recant or else you slay mee." This, though, is a repetition and may be a copyist's error.

Were either of these settings used in the original productions of the play? There is little evidence, other than the similarities of the texts and the proximity of the dates of the first version and the play, to suggest that either setting was known to Shakespeare. On the other hand, it seems quite probable that the *melody* or tune of the song is that used when the song was heard on Shakespeare's stage. The artistic structure of the song indicates, as we have previously noted, that it was originally set to a specific melody which probably remained essentially unaltered as long as the song was performed. The irregular length of the musical lines including the interjections and questions would seem to require a more specialized setting than a typical ballad whose lyrics might well be sung to any one of several tunes. The fact that the melody remains the same, though it appears in versions apparently made independently by different composers separated in time by several decades, should support the belief that the melody was as much the same when heard on the stage in 1611 or 1613.

The failure of both manuscripts to show any associations of the musical settings with the play might also imply that neither the music nor the lyrics were the peculiar property of Shakespeare. He might have chosen from a common fund of popular ayres a dialogue song so familiar that "there's scarse a Maide westward but she sings it" and inserted it at the appropriate point in the play. This would not have been an unusual practice on his part. The ayre in *As You Like It,* "It was a Lover and his Lass," is believed by Edmund Fellowes to have been a popular song adapted independently by Shakespeare and Thomas Morley, who gave it a musical setting.[19] And, of course, Robert Jones' ayre, "Farewell, Dear Love," was adapted by Shakespeare for use in *Twelfth Night,* II, iii.[20]

After the dialogue song, Autolycus, the Clown, and the "Wenches" move offstage to haggle over the peddler's wares. As our rascal exits, he sings another vender's cry, "Will you buy any Tape, or Lace for your Cape?" Music for this song is missing, but the song belongs, as does "Lawne as white as driven Snow," to a genre frequently found in the early song books. For practical purposes, in Figure 31 the song is set to an old ballad tune, "Sellenger's Round," as found in The Fitzwilliam Virginal Book and reproduced in Chappell's *Old English Popular Music,* I, 256, Gibbon's *Melody and the Lyric,* p. 52, and elsewhere.

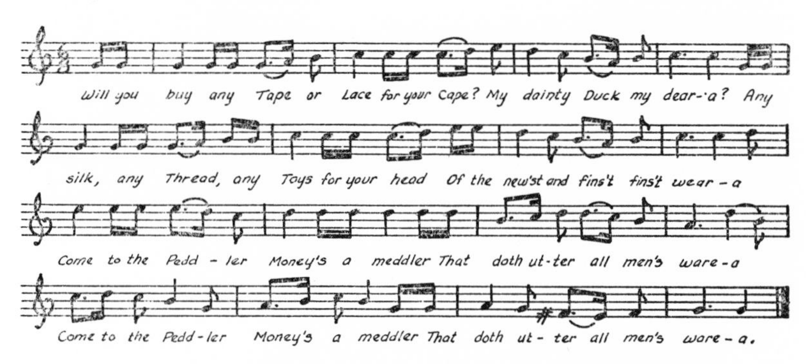

FIGURE 31.—Will you buy any Tape, or Lace for your Cape?

This is the final song sung by Autolycus. In recapitulation it appears that he has sung six songs within the relatively short time taken by two scenes, one of them quite brief. These songs include a spring song, or "reverdie," and two "strolling songs" (probably all three in ballad form); a peddler's cry which, if Wilson's setting is good evidence, was a sophisticated version of a popular type; a dialogue song in imitation of a folk type; and a final peddler's cry which also may have been set to some lutenist's ayre.

The types of songs assigned Autolycus, the extravagant praise accorded the singer by the servant, and the court fool-singer combination all suggest that the actor who played the part of Autolycus in the original production of the play must have been an experienced actor-singer on whom the King's Men could rely to set the pace for the concluding part of the play. Who could that have been but Robert Armin, last observed as Feste in *Twelfth Night?* He was still with the King's Men, presumably a shareholder, and was still taking comedy roles. He was listed as a comedian in the cast of Jonson's *The Alchemist,* first performed a few weeks before October, 1610.[21] Perhaps the nature of Shakespeare's middle comedies was not such to provide Armin with the parts in which he excelled; and perhaps it was only in this one of the final comedies that he found a congenial part. If Armin did play Autolycus, it is pleasant to note that his part provided him a fitting swan's song. After this performance he disappears from Shakespeare's plays.

With the departure of Autolycus, the play turns from song back to the dance.

Servant. Mayster, there is three Carters, three Shepherds, three Swineherds y have made themselves all men of haire, they cal themselves Saltiers, and they have a Dance, which the Wenches say is a gallymaufrey of Gambols, because they are not in't but they themselves are o'th' minde (if it bee not too rough for some, that know little but bowling) it will please plentifully.

* * * * * * * * *

One three of them, by their owne report (Sir,)
hath danc'd before the King: and not the worst
of the three, but iumpes twelve foote and a halfe
by th' squire.

* * * * * * * * *

Heere a Dance of twelve Satyres.

Parrott sees little dramatic value in this dance and suggests that it is a later interpolation.[22] Yet when we consider its use in the masque-within-the-play, we may have some mental reservations on this point. Also if we note the masques and the pastoral plays, such as *The Maids Metamorphosis, Wily Beguiled, Summers Last Will and Testament, The Golden Age,* and *The Silver Age,* all of whose performances surrounded the first production of *The Winter's Tale,* other reasons for the dance become apparent, if not its dramatic value. It was fashionable at this time, as the cited productions indicate, to turn the stage over to nymphs and satyrs, shepherds and shepherdesses; hence, the dance would be a concession to fashion—a necessary part of the setting and spectacle—which Shakespeare's skill made an integral part of the play. At the same time we may note that the spectacle and songs, including the dance of the satyrs, prolong the suspense from the time Florizel and Perdita reveal their love until, after this dance, Polixenes throws off his disguise and prevents the contracting of the lovers.

The performance of the dance is described in some detail by the servant who introduces it. Certainly it was by Jacobean court standards a wild, grotesque dance marked by great leaps into the air. Yet we should not be misled by a modern sense of realism. Probably the hairy men here presented a dance almost as artificial and formal as the euphuistic literature whence it was derived.

Thomas Ravenscroft supplies us with the music of a satyrs' dance as the Jacobean courtiers and ladies doubtless saw it performed. In his *A Briefe Discourse* (1614), p. 3, he explains that the dances he includes as examples are

> *Dauncing,* but that with some difference from the common *Exercise* now a daies of it, in our *Maskes* and *Revells:* as not grounded on the *Dauncing of Measures,* and accordingly bound to some particular *Rules* and *Numbers,* proper to the *Nature* of that *Daunce* only, which then is afoot: But fashioned like those *Antique Daunces,* which the *Poets* would have us beleeve, the *Fayries,* and the *Satyres,* and those other *Rurall Natures* frequented, and having in them, much more *variety* and *change* then any other *Composition,* and withall so expressing our *imperfect Moods* and *Measures.* . . .

Thus, Ravenscroft makes a distinction between the formal dance types performed by the Revellers in the masques—the pavanes, galliards, almains, *et al.*—and the fantastic dances usually presented by professional dancers. The former were each usually limited to one time signature (4/4, 3/4, or 6/8) and to one key, whereas the *"Antique"* dances in each case might contain several "changes" in both time and key.

As an example Ravenscroft included a *Satyres Daunce* with lyric, making it a dance-song (see Fig. 32). He probably wrote it for one of the choirboy plays, as he was a graduate of the St. Paul's Children and afterwards remained closely associated with the company.[23] While the music is wild only in its use of *"imperfect Moods and Measures,"* the measures containing the held whole notes would provide time for several leaps and, perhaps, some extempore footwork outside the regular pattern of the dance.

John Cutts believes that the "Satyres Masque" shown in the Appendix is by Robert Johnson, who wrote it for Jonson's masque, *Oberon.* He then states, "This music was transferred immediately to the original performance of 'The Winter's Tale.'" But Cutts presents no evidence of this transfer other than the statement that

FIGURE 32.—Satyres Daunce

the dance is "in keeping with the mood of the play" (see his "Robert Johnson: King's Musician . . . ," pp. 110-125). The article presents some invaluable material on the music in the last three of Shakespeare's comedies. Ravenscroft's music is used as an illustration in Figure 32 for the practical reason that Ravenscroft supplies four parts readily available. Edward Dent has supplied inner voices for the "Satyres Masque" (Cutts, *op. cit.*, n. 8), but his setting is apparently unpublished.

The satyrs' dance provides a fitting musical climax for the scene; with the bitter denunciation of the lovers by Polixenes, the festival ends and music is heard no more until by its mystic power Hermione is turned in the next act from a statue into a loving wife.

Many commentators on the play have noted that the final scene, indeed the final act, is a skillful preparation for the transformation episode, and there is no doubt that the result is highly effective. In keeping with his frequent use of music to underscore dramatic climaxes, Shakespeare calls for music at this point. The music is also a mark of the supernatural; its magical powers revive Hermione, just as the music called for by Cerimon restored life to Thaisa in *Pericles.* Of course, we know that Paulina has stationed musicians nearby to supply the music she later calls for, but it does not disturb us. We like to watch the magician even though we know his tricks. To Leontes and his party the transformation is a tender marvel.

Paulina approaches the "statue"; she calls for silence, then raises her hand.

> *Paul.* Musick; awake her: Strike:
> 'Tis time: descend: be Stone no more: approach
> Strike all that looke upon with mervaile: Come:
> Ile fill your Grave up: stirre: nay, come away:
> Bequeath to Death your numnesse: (for from him,
> Deare Life redeemes you) you perceive she stirres. . . .

The punctuation of these lines indicates that the awakening of Hermione is a gradual one. Paulina's commands are seemingly spoken between rather long pauses during which the mysterious music could be heard with great effect. The solemn tones were probably provided by a consort of viols: the command "Strike" was usually associated with string instruments. The music should cease, perhaps, when Leontes clasps Hermione's hand in his. Antony Holborne's *Pavanes, galliards, almains* . . . (1599) again provides the treble and bass parts of a consort piece appropriately entitled "Posthuma," which seems fitting here (see Fig. 33).

FIGURE 33.—Posthuma

G. Wilson Knight in his study of Shakespeare's symbolism and imagery (*The Crown of Life,* pp. 18, 19) has this to say about the music in this scene and in the similar scene in *Pericles:*

This music may seem to perform a dual function: first, to suggest, as a symbol of pure aesthetic delight, the nature of the act (resurrection and reunion) being performed; second, to anaesthetize the critical faculty, as does the overture in a theatre, and prepare the mind for some extraordinary event. But these are in reality twin aspects of the same function: for music, like erotic sight, raises the consciousness until it is in tune with a reality beyond the reach of wisdom . . . Music in Shakespeare is ever the solace and companion of love, and love in Shakespeare the language of mysticism.

Such thoughts probably did not enter the minds of the gorgeously attired courtiers, ladies-in-waiting, noblemen, and ladies who were charmed by the simplicity of this pastoral-masque-fairy-tale with its true lovers, cruel parents, and magic spells. But they must have been delighted by the freshness which Shakespeare's characters brought to the slightly tarnished classical props of the masques, and by the color and spectacle these props assumed when placed within Shakespeare's poetic enchantment. Yet we would do well to note the musical symbolism, because we shall observe Shakespeare, with its aid, turning another winter's tale into the beautiful and infinite allegory which is *The Tempest.*

Notes

1. *Shakespeare: Twenty-Three Plays . . .*, p. 1011.
2. See Chapter I and also J. Long, *Shakespeare's Use of Music,* I.
3. E. Chambers, *The Elizabethan Stage,* I, 172.
4. *Ibid.,* pp. 173, 174.
5. *Ibid.,* p. 173.
6. *Ibid.,* p. 170.
7. Note especially *The Maid's Metamorphosis* (1600), *Wily Beguiled* (1606), Nashe's *Summer's Last Will and Testament* (1600), Heywood's *The Golden Age* (1611) and *The Silver Age* (1613), and most of Marston's plays.
8. H. Evans, *English Masques,* pp. 58-71; P. Vivian (ed.), *Campion's Works,* pp. 89-100; A. Thorndike, *The Influence of Beaumont and Fletcher on Shakespeare,* pp. 32, 33.
9. "Some Musical Aspects of the English Court Masque," pp. 3-19.
10. Vivian, *op. cit.*
11. Evans, *op. cit.*
12. First Folio text used throughout this chapter.
13. See W. Chappell, *Old English Popular Music,* I, 127, 128.
14. H. Furness, Variorum edition, p. 166, n. 24.
15. "An Unpublished Contemporary Setting . . .," pp. 86-89.
16. Microfilm furnished me by the New York Public Library.
17. "An Unpublished Contemporary Setting . . .," p. 86.
18. Microfilm furnished me by the New York Public Library.
19. See Morley, *The First Booke of Airs* as reprinted in Fellowes, *The English School of Lutenist Song Writers,* 1st Series, No. 16, particularly n. VI; p. 26; and p. 28, n.
20. Long, *Shakespeare's Use of Music,* I, 173.
21. B. Jonson, *Ben Jonson,* IX, 223-225.
22. *Op. cit.,* p. 1010.
23. W. Lawrence, "Thomas Ravenscroft's Theatrical Association," pp. 418-423.

SEVEN

The Tempest

ITH *The Tempest* WE REACH THE FINAL, GREAT comedy—great not only for its brave new world of love and harmony, for its surges of language, but great also because it is both summation and recapitulation. It is as though Shakespeare by some alchemical process had taken his noblest thoughts, clothed them in glowing words, and then by the Orphic power of music had shaped them into a lump of gold capable of infinite allegorical forms. For *The Tempest* is a complex of delights—the enchantment and poetry of *A Midsummer Night's Dream,* the romance of *As You Like It,* the philosophy of *Hamlet,* the comedy and good nature of *The Winter's Tale,* the music and spectacle of many plays, and an allegorical puzzle that infects the imagination and makes every reading of the play a new delight.

Amid such plenty it is impossible to compartmentalize the different functions of the music in the play. The very quantity of the music poses a problem. Perhaps we might consider the subject by moving from the general to the particular in four steps. In the first two we shall consider the external factors influencing the use and performance of the music and the comprehensive purposes of the music within the play as a whole. With this preparation we shall then be ready, in the last two steps, to pursue our main object, the functions of the music in particular episodes in the play, and the music itself and its performance. Of course, in such a scheme some overlapping is inevitable, but perhaps the need for clarity is sufficient excuse.

The Occasion for The Tempest

The salient fact concerning the two earliest recorded performances of the play is that it was produced at Whitehall for the Court.

The first performance occurred in 1611; the second was a revival of the play as part of the festivities celebrating the marriage in February, 1613, of Frederick, Count Palatine, and Princess Elizabeth of England. *The Tempest* was one of fourteen plays given during the celebration. Apparently little or no revision was made in the script of the play before its second production. It has been suggested that the masque of Juno and Ceres was added by another hand the better to adapt the play to a royal wedding, but Chambers believes that only the song in the masque may be non-Shakespearean.[1] It seems reasonable to agree that the Folio 1623 text is that used for the court performance, with perhaps the addition of Prospero's epilogue when and if the play was later produced in the public playhouse.

When Shakespeare wrote the play, however, he clearly had a court performance in mind. The romantic plot of the lovers, the allegorical overtones, the spectacle and music of the work, all point to a courtly audience and elaborate stage facilities. In this respect we are reminded of *A Midsummer Night's Dream* which, as we remember, was writen for a similar occasion, although for a simpler stage.

For the reasons discussed in the preceding chapter, the influence of the masque is strongly marked in this comedy. The occasional nature of the play, the spectacle, and especially the allegory, are reflections of the masques, some of which were being performed at the same time and in the same hall in 1613. Certainly Shakespeare would have thought much about the masques and would have considered the extra musicians, dancers, scenic effects, and costumes that he could draw upon for a royal command performance.

The masque influence is clearly apparent in *The Tempest;* but no restriction of the music and dance to one part of the play occurs in this case. Rather, these elements pervade the fabric of the play, are woven into its texture. In a sense this is a return to the earlier habits of Shakespeare, but the quantity of music in *The Tempest* is so great, and its use so frequent and surrounded with such spectacle, that one wonders whether it is a play using masque elements or a dramatized masque. Shakespeare probably did not stop to consider the question. He was writing what perhaps he believed was his last play. Naturally he would want to make a grand exit from the stage which he considered synonymous with life. In order to do so, he said what he wanted to say and employed every means at his disposal to help him say it. How fortunate that he found both words and stage large enough for his purpose at the climax of his career! And how fortunate that he had an audience that evoked and appreciated the fantasy and symbolism which enabled him to transcend the limitations of even the great Whitehall Banqueting House!

The Comprehensive Functions of the Music

Three distinct, though intertwined, dramatic conventions explain the comprehensive purposes of the music. One of these is, of course, the intrinsic pleasure afforded by the music. Ordinarily the plays written for the public playhouses did not emphasize music as an end in itself: the expense of hiring extra musicians, the relatively short time available for the performance of a play, the quality of the audience, all these factors threw emphasis on swift action, a tight plot, dramatic economy, and the use of as small a company of hired men as possible.

These restrictions were largely removed on those occasions when the King's Men shifted their stage from the Globe to Blackfriars or to the Court. Perhaps following the example set by the choirboy companies, the King's Men began to use more music in the plays produced on the private stages. Much of this music was still functional in nature—habit is hard to break—but it seems logical to assume that the players would also consider the songs and dances as having high intrinsic value to their refined court audiences. Moreover, in an atmosphere of masque entertainments the King's Men might be expected to provide music of equal quality. None of the music in *The Tempest,* with the possible exception of the masque song of Juno and Ceres mentioned earlier, can be considered as inserted for its musical value alone. Yet the settings made by Robert Johnson of "Full Fathom Five" and "Where the Bee Sucks," presumably for the 1613 revival of the play, are still charming and artful pieces of music.

The second comprehensive function of the music is purely symbolic. For this purpose also, it was necessary that the music be, for the most part, high in esthetic quality and performed with considerable art.

Any enveloping symbolism of the play will rest on the allegorical interpretation of it made by the reader. Let us consider the comedy an allegory of universal love, by whose power the tempests of men's lives and natures are calmed and the discordant elements present in both man and his world finally achieve a reconciliation and a harmony.[2] Let us consider the play as some great plagal cadence whose passing chords are resolved by the soul-satisfying completeness and finality of the tonic chord. It requires no great synthesis to equate Love with Harmony, Harmony with Music, Music with Divinity, if we consider at the same time all of the ideas associated by Shakespeare with each of these terms and if we recall the musical symbolism accepted by Mersenne and Barnes. Thus, as an overarching symbol Music is Harmony, which is Love, the perfected relationship between man and himself, man and his fellow men, man and woman, man and his universe, and man and God.

The test of this symbolism, of course, is its applicability in a consistent manner to the episodes involving music, and the integration of each incident into an allegorical interpretation of the whole play. Such a treatment of the music in the play has been done, in part, by G. Wilson Knight in his books, *The Crown of Life* and *The Shakespearian Tempest.* We need not duplicate here what he has already attempted, but when we turn to specific incidents in the play, we may find some concrete examples of musical symbolism which are beyond the scope of Knight's discussion.

Symbolism is closely allied to fantasy, and fantasy to the supernatural. All three represent an attempt to transcend creatively the limitations of the natural world. In *The Tempest* the dramatic conflict is basically the conflict between the godlike nature of man and the bestial nature of man. Taking sides in this metaphysical struggle are the supernatural forces—the Dominations, Powers, and elemental spirits of Neo-Platonic origin—represented by Prospero's magic, Ariel, and the assorted spirits of earth, water, air, and fire commanded by Ariel, all of whom urge the mortals toward divinity. Caliban urges them toward bestiality. Thus, the play is filled with various charms, enchantments, and other supernatural phenomena, all of which require the use of music to represent the supernatural—the third comprehensive function of the music.

When we recall the consistent use of music by Shakespeare to accompany and to enhance the mystery of scenes containing gods, goddesses, spirits, fairies, and ghosts, we may comprehend the importance of music in the strange events which occur on Prospero's magic isle. Where there is magic, there is music. No wonder that even the clod-like Caliban is dimly aware of the music surrounding him and that the oafish Stephano can exclaim, "This will prove a brave kingdome to me,/ Where I shall have my Musicke for nothing."

So far we have dealt largely with generalities, but general statements are risky unless they can be shown to rest on solid evidence. It is time, therefore, that we turn to specific evidence in the play.

The Specific Functions of the Music

The harmonic structure of Prospero's island first becomes audible in the scene (I, ii) following the tempest which casts the party of noblemen upon the shore. Ferdinand by the magical power of Prospero is separated from his father and comrades and is alone near the sea's edge. When he wanders onto the stage, still dazed by his miraculous rescue, his attention has already been claimed by ethereal music performed by Ariel, whose song is accompanied by a distant barking of dogs and crowing of cocks. Ariel, addressing unseen spirits, sings:

Enter Ferdinand & Ariel, invisible playing & singing.

Ariel Song. *Come unto these yellow sands,*
and then take hands:
Curtsied when you have, and kist
the wilde waves whist:

Foote it featly heere, and there, and sweete Sprights
beare th burthen. Burthen dispersedly
Harke, harke, bowgh wawgh: the watch-Dogges barke,
bowgh-wawgh

Ar. *Hark, hark, I heare, the straine of strutting Chanticlere*
cry cockadidle-dowe.

Fer. Where shold this Musick be? I'th aire, or th'earth?
It sounds no more: and sure it waytes upon
Some God 'oth'Iland, sitting on a banke,
Weeping againe the King my Fathers wracke,
This Musicke crept by me upon the waters,
Allaying both their fury, and my passion
With it's sweet ayre: thence I have follow'd it
(Or it hath drawne me rather) but 'tis gone.
No, it begins againe.

Ariell Song. *Full fadom five thy Father lies,*
Of his bones are Corrall made:
Those are pearles that were his eies,
Nothing of him that doth fade,
But doth suffer a Sea-change
Into something rich, & strange:
Sea: Nimphs hourly ring his knell.
Burthen: ding dong.
Harke now I heare them, ding-dong bell.

Fer. The Ditty do's remember my drown'd father,
This is no mortall business, nor no sound
That the earth owes: I heare it now above me.

Pro. The fringed Curtaines of thine eye advance;
And say what thou see'st yond.

Mira. What is't a Spirit?
Lord, how it lookes about: Beleeve me sir,
It carries a brave forme. But 'tis a spirit.

* * * * * * *

I might call him
A thing divine, for nothing naturall
I ever saw so Noble.

* * * * * * *

Fer. Most sure the Godesse
On whom these ayres attend. . . .[3]

This lengthy quotation is made because both songs and the musical modulation between them form a dramatic and esthetic unity. First, let us consider the supernatural quality of the music. The songs proceed from Ariel and his accompanying sprites, but there is also music from "above me," as Ferdinand remarks. Actually, this music is Prospero's magic made manifest. By his mysterious power Prospero has evoked the tempest. Once its purpose has been accomplished, Prospero calms the storm and enchants both Miranda and Ferdinand; so when they meet they immediately fall in love. The two songs and their instrumental support are the audible aspects of this gentler magic.

First the calming of the tempest. Evidently the storm continues into Scene ii, until Ariel sings his first song, "Come unto these yellow sands." Earlier Miranda refers to the tempest (lines 174-176), when she asks Prospero, "And now I pray you Sir,/ For still 'tis beating in my minde; your reason/ For raysing this Sea-storme?" By means of the song Ariel, in the form of a sea-spirit, directs his attendant spirits to curtsy and to kiss the "wilde waves whist." Ferdinand tells us, following the song, that this music "crept by me upon the waters,/ Allaying both their fury, and my passion/ With it's sweet ayre. . . ." Thus, it is clear that the music calms the storm.

There is more to this charm. By its power Ferdinand is brought into the presence of Miranda. Ferdinand says of the song, "thence have I follow'd it/ (Or it hath drawne me rather). . . ." The music-magic is still operating. By means of the gentle, consoling elegy which now is heard by Ferdinand, the prince's grief for his lost father is soothed; by the time he becomes aware of Miranda, he is prepared for another emotion, his love of Miranda.[4]

Music leads Ferdinand to Miranda, and it is directly responsible for their love at first sight; for Prospero's enchantment, we remember, is still in force. This is indicated by the fact that this tender meeting is underscored by music. As the distant tolling of the sea-nymphs' knell dies away, Ferdinand exclaims in wonder, "The Ditty do's remember my drown'd father,/ This is no mortall busines, nor no sound/ That the earth owes: I heare it now above me." Hence, the music continues, although it probably changes to a more lyrical, less solemn, quality. Against this melodic background the lovers' eyes first meet.

The direct connection, and result, of this dramatic event and the melody which envelopes it, is interesting. Miranda, perceiving Ferdinand, believes him to be of divine origin, for she says, "I might call him/ A thing divine, for nothing naturall/ I ever saw so Noble." Ferdinand likewise believes Miranda is a divinity, and he associates her with the mysterious music he hears around him. "Most sure the Goddesse/ On whom these ayres attend. . . ." We therefore observe a direct linking of music with harmony, love, and divinity, the true source of Prospero's enchantments.

Now we are beginning to talk in symbolic terms again. In order to observe the symbolism of this musical episode completely, however, we must retrace our steps and join Ferdinand as he sits on the seashore weeping for the presumed loss of his father. He is diverted by Ariel's song and the echoing voices of the spirits who dance around him. These spirits are apparently earth-spirits of a fairly domestic nature. The watchdogs' and the cocks' voices represent the outposts of human society to which Ferdinand is returning and the familiar order and peace which the weary traveler finds upon return to his home.

The voices that sing from the sea the lovely knell for Alonso, however, are water-spirits (perhaps Plotinian) who, though apparently responsible for Alonso's death, yet make the separation of the King and his son as merciful as possible. Both the symbolism of the play and Shakespeare's plot require that Ferdinand should temporarily believe his father dead, but the symbolism also requires that Ferdinand should suffer no real harm in the process. He cannot know true harmony until he has experienced dissonance; hence, the tempest subsides to music, Ferdinand is returned to human society, his grief assuaged, and his love for Miranda evoked by divine music. All is for the present harmonious in nature, in Ferdinand, and between Prospero, Ferdinand, and Miranda.

Now let us look at this same episode through more prosaic eyes. When Shakespeare began to write the play, he apparently determined to abide by the classic concept of unity of time, that is, to restrict the action of the play within twelve hours. This he did, but in so doing he had to use some legerdemain of his own. In this case he had to calm the storm, show us a grief-stricken Ferdinand, transport him from the seashore into the presence of Miranda, erase his woe, and then have him fall totally in love with Miranda—all to be done in the shortest possible time and without the rapid sequence of events seeming improbable. Shakespeare used the songs and music here to create the desired illusion. While we listen to the songs, we are not conscious of time; consequently, when the action resumes we do not recall the lapse of time. Shakespeare has telescoped the passage of time without our being aware of what has happened. The music has thus contributed to the dramatic unity of the play.

The scene now shifts to another part of the island where the weary and grieving Alonso and Gonzalo, his trusted counselor, fall into a deep sleep brought on by Ariel administering Prospero's charm. While they slumber, Antonio and Sebastian plot to murder them (II, i). The charm, of course, is set to music.

Enter Ariell playing solemne Musicke.

* * * * * * * *

Gon. . . . Will you laugh me asleepe, for I am very heavy.
Ant. Go sleepe, and heare us.
Alon. What, all so soone asleepe? I with mine eyes
Would (with themselves) shut up my thoughts,
I find they are inclin'd to do so.

After Alonso also falls asleep, Antonio and Sebastian prepare to murder both of them.

Ant. Draw together;
And when I reare my hand, do you the like
To fall it on *Gonzalo*.
Seb. O, but one word.

Enter Ariell with Musicke and Song.
Ariel. My Master through his Art foresees the danger
That you (his friend) are in, and sends me forth
(For else his proiect dies) to keepe them living.
Sings in Gonzaloes eare.

While you here do snoaring lie,
Open-ey'd Conspiracie
His time doth take:
If of Life you keepe a care,
Shake off slumber and beware
Awake, Awake.

Ant. Then let us both be sodaine.
Gon. Now, good Angels preserve the King.

Through the timely intervention of Ariel the King is spared to go safely on to seek his son.

In these two musical incidents our Music-Harmony-Love-Divinity symbol is again applicable. The "solemne Musicke" which lulls Alonso and Gonzalo to sleep serves a purpose similar to that of the elegy heard by Ferdinand; that is, it knits up the King's ravel'd sleave of care. As Sebastian says, "[Sleep] seldome visits sorrow, when it doth, it is a Comforter." The slumber music is thus a merciful gesture made by Prospero. Since music induces the slumber, music must end it; and this is the purpose of the song, as Ariel carefully tells us. The warning is an example of Prospero's love for Alonso and, especially, for Gonzalo who had shown mercy to Prospero and the infant Miranda. We note that the warning is given to Gonzalo, not to the King. We also observe that "good Angels" do preserve the King by means of Ariel's song. Our symbolic parallel is thus completed.

In the next musical scene the obverse of this symbolism is presented. Stephano, reeling ripe with wine, staggers onto the scene (II, ii) wherein he, Trinculo, and Caliban form their stupid and vicious alliance against Prospero.

Enter Stephano singing.

Ste. *I shall no more to sea, to sea, here shall I dye ashore.*
This is a very scurvy tune to sing at a mans
Funerall: well, here's my comfort. Drinkes.
Sings. *The Master, the Swabber, the Boate-swaine & I;*
The Gunner, and his Mate
Lov'd Mall, Meg and Marrian, and Margerie,
But none of us car'd for Kate.
For she had a tongue with a tang,

Would cry to a Sailor goe hang:
She lov'd not the savour of Tar nor of Pitch,
Yet a Tailor might scratch her where ere she did itch,
Then to Sea Boyes, and let her goe hang.
This is a scurvy tune too:
But here's my comfort. *drinks.*

Of course, Stephano sings because he is drunk, but the nature of both the singer and the song reveals symbolic connotations. In contrast to the spirit-music provided by Ariel, this is a "scurvy tune" sung by a carnal oaf much befuddled by drink. The bawdy song, the gross nature of Stephano, his drunkenness—all these reveal in the character of Stephano (and also, as we shall later discover, Trinculo and Caliban) the earthiness, sensuality, and disharmony personified by these opponents of Prospero's refined reign. We soon learn that all three are fit only for spoils and stratagems. They are parts of the inharmonious element of the island, and the sea-chantey accents their qualities.

Caliban, the only near-human creature lower than Stephano and Trinculo in the chain of creation, soon gilds himself with the celestial liquor borne by Stephano. In his drunken condition, delighted by the license promised him by his new god, Caliban bursts into song.

Caliban Sings drunkenly.
Farewell Master: farewell, farewell.
Tri. A howling Monster: a drunken Monster.
Cal. No more dams I'le make for fish,
Nor fetch in firing, at requiring,
Nor scrape trenchering, nor wash dish,
Ban' ban' Cacal, ban
Has a new Master, get a new Man.

Here again the music is used to suggest license and lack of harmony rather than form and harmony. Caliban cannot sing as does Ariel, or even Stephano. What he "howls," as Trinculo describes his performance, is a strange doggerel quite different from the music heard previously in the play.

Later (III, ii), the three complete their plan to murder Prospero, ravish Miranda, and become kings of the island.

Cal. Thou mak'st me merry: I am full of pleasure,
Let us be iocond. Will you troule the Catch
You taught me but whileare?
Ste. At thy request Monster, I will do reason,
Any reason: Come on *Trinculo,* let us sing.
Sings.
Flout 'em, and cout'em: skowt'em, and flout 'em.
Thought is free.
Cal. That's not the tune.
Ariell plaies the tune on a Tabor and Pipe.
Ste. What's this same?
Trin. This is the tune of our Catch, plaid by the picture of Nobody.

* * * * * * * *

Trin. The sound is going away;
Lets follow it, and after do our worke.
Ste. Leade Monster,
Wee'l follow: I would I could see this Taborer,
He layes it on.

Having heard some samples of Stephano's and Caliban's singing, we should not be surprised that, with Trinculo, they cannot sing even the simplest kind of part-song, the "catch." Individually they cannot sing, collectively they achieve no harmony nor even carry a tune—a foreshadowing of their failure to work in concert toward carrying out their plot. Ariel has to play the tune for them; and since, musically, he controls the situation, he uses his power to divert the three from their goal. Following Ariel's piping, they are led off on a wild-goose chase.

Thus, in the music associated with Stephano, Trinculo, and Caliban we have the lower notes of Mersenne's gamut personified, and through this personification we have a telling piece of characterization. Lust, license, unreasoning obedience to sensuality, and incoherence are mirrored by the bawling and howling, and finally by the chaos which marks the music attempted by the three sots.

In III, iii, the supernatural music reappears. The party of noblemen are suddenly confronted by a banquet spread before them in a mysterious manner.

Solemne and strange Musicke: and Prosper on the top (invisible:) Enter severall strange shapes, bringing in a Banket; and dance about it with gentle actions of salutations, and inviting the King, &c to eate, they depart.

Al. What harmony is this? my good friends, harke.
Gon. Marvellous sweet Musicke

The hungry noblemen comment on this apparition and, after the strange servitors disappear, attempt to eat the food spread before them. Before they can taste it, Ariel in the form of a harpy causes the food to disappear. He then lectures the noblemen on the injustice done Prospero and Miranda. Only "hearts-sorrow and a cleere life ensuing" can ransom them from the consequences of their past sins. As Ariel ends his oration, the shapes reappear and remove the banquet table.

He vanishes in Thunder: then (to soft Musicke) Enter the shapes againe, and daunce (with mockes and mowes) and carrying out the Table.

Knight, in *The Crown of Life*, pp. 215, 216, interprets this mock-repast as symbolizing the separation of the noblemen from humane society as a result of their inhumanity to Prospero and his daughter. Ariel's tongue-lashing seems to support this interpretation. The music apparently identifies the strange shapes with the beneficent power which operates in other incidents where solemn or sweet music is heard. Magic of course we expect to be accompanied by music. This interlude also provides the illusion which covers the setting of the stage for the spectacular banquet. The table and its contents must be placed on the stage and then later removed. Obviously on a magic island spirits may turn stagehands or *vice versa.* Spirits, pantomime, and music serve the purpose, and the table appears and disappears as though by magic.

This bit of stage spectacle is a taste of the more impressive dramatic fare found later in the masque of Juno, Iris, and Ceres (IV, i). This nuptial tribute is an epithalamium serving the same beneficent purpose as the fairy blessing at the end of *A Midsummer*

Night's Dream. "Soft musick" sounds as Iris enters the scene and continues until Juno descends and joins Ceres in their wedding hymn.

They Sing.

Ju. Honor, riches, marriage, blessing:
Long continuance and encreasing,
Hourely joyes, be still upon you,
Iuno sings her blessings on you.
Earths increase, foyzon plentie,
Barnes, and Garners, never empty;
Vines, with clustring bunches growing,
Plants, with goodly burthen bowing:
Spring come to you at the farthest,
In the very end of Harvest.
Scarcity and want shall shun you,
Ceres' blessing so is on you.

Fer. This is most maiesticke vision, and
Harmonious charmingly: . . .

* * * * * * *

Let me live here ever,
So rare a wondred Father, and a wife
Makes this place Paradise.

Hardly have the two goddesses ended their song when the stage is filled with nymphs and reapers.

Enter certaine Reapers (properly habited:) they ioyne with the Nimphes, in a gracefull dance, towards the end whereof, Prospero *starts sodainly and speakes, after which to a strange hollow and confused noyse, they heavily vanish.*

Pro. I had forgot that foule conspiracy
Of the beast Calliban, and his confederates
Against my life: the minute of their plot
Is almost come: Well done, avoid: no more.

This masque episode must have been highly effective in its original staging. Prospero by his power creates a tangible memory of the Golden Age when men lived in peace with Nature, which showered its bounty upon them, when mortal reapers could join hands with the nymphs in a dance set to the rhythm of the seasons. Here is another vision of the brave new world that Ferdinand, fascinated, believes a paradise. Prospero is himself bemused by the vision. Here is what his books tell him the world could and should be. How fair, how pleasant, how innocent!

But Prospero is too wise to be fooled even by himself. His thoughts suddenly turn to the snakes in Ferdinand's Paradise—Caliban and his crew. Perhaps it is the sudden and overwhelming contrast between the ideal and the immediate that moves Prospero so to passion and to break off the Reapers' dance, to exclaim sadly as the "shadows" disappear, "These our actors, (As I foretold you) were all Spirits, and/ Are melted into Ayre, into thin Ayre. . . ."

The Elector and Princess Elizabeth were no doubt pleased with the courtly tribute paid them by Shakespeare and by the artistic music which such a tribute would demand. No doubt the music was designed to provide a lyrical background to the speeches of the goddesses as well as to weave a web of mystery and awe around them. It probably did not occur to the royal minds that the celestial airs also covered the noise made by Juno's descent, either on a lift or down a flight of stairs.

The "strange hollow and confused noyse" to which the actors in the masque disappear requires an attempt at explanation. The stage direction may refer to the noise of the machinery that lowered the dancers through one or more trap doors in the stage floor. Yet it does not seem probable that such a disturbance would have been permitted by the players. If another meaning for "noyse" be recalled, that is, a band of musicians playing with inferior skill, or the music played by such musicians, then we might assume that consort music was played to cover the sound of the stage machinery. Not knowing the score used, or that music was actually used, we cannot determine what music was played; but we can note another reason why such "noyse" may have been used if we recall the symbolism in the play.

With the disappearance of the idealized pageantry of the masque as a result of Prospero's thought of Caliban, the music undergoes a change from the graceful measures of the dance to the "confused" (or could it have been "discordant"?) music to which the masque disappears. The celestial vision is replaced by the harsh recollection of brutish conspiracy. If the symbolism is to remain consistent, would not the music have reflected the discord in Prospero's harmonious vision? And if strictly from a dramatic point of view Shakespeare had to abbreviate the normal masque structure, would this not be an effective way to interrupt it? As a beautiful but fragile piece of glass shattered by a blow, Prospero's vision vanishes in a swirl of broken harmony.

This would be the last harsh music heard in the play. Prospero counters the plot. With all the storm-tossed mortals now in his power, he decides that "the rarer Action is/ In vertue, then in vengeance." Satisfied of their true penitence, he sees his task ended and without regret gives up his magical powers.

> But this rough Magicke
> I heere abiure: and when I have requir'd
> Some heavenly Musicke (which even now I do)
> To work mine end upon their Sences, that
> This Ayrie-charme is for, I'le breake my staffe,
> Bury it certain fadomes in the earth,
> And deeper then did ever Plummet sound
> Ile drowne my booke.
>
> *Solemne musicke.*

This solemn music brings the enchanted noblemen into Prospero's presence, and while it suspends their senses, it also paradoxically "cures" them. Prospero refers to this phenomenon when he remarks of the music, "A solemne Ayre, and the best comforter,/ To an unsettled fancie, Cure thy braines/ (Now useless) boile within thy skull." One by one he restores each stricken man to his senses. This is not quickly done, however. Prospero notes that "Their understanding/ Begins to swell, and the approching tide/ Will shortly fill the reasonable shore/ That now ly foule and muddy. . . ." The music probably continues as long as Prospero's charm lasts. It thus underscores the dramatic climax of the play, provides audible magic, cures the irrational quality of the noblemen's minds (by implication the source of their evil actions), and symbolizes the restored harmony of human relationships. We should not overlook Shakespeare's metaphor wherein the "understanding" is spoken of as a sea—the sea which was formerly tempest-tossed but now is controlled by the tidal influence of the moon. And by the term "understanding," could Shakespeare have meant the *Entendement* of Mersenne?

The world of magic dissolves when Prospero removes his robe. This ritualistic act is performed in the sight of the audience and involves a break in the action of the play. Ariel's song "Where the Bee Sucks" fills this break until Prospero is once again as he "was sometime Millaine," and the action can resume.

With the lifting of the clouds from the moral and rational qualities of the King and his party, Nature is once more harmonious. The solemn music gives way to the happy caroling of Ariel as he bursts into his lovely air. Not only is he aware of his approaching freedom, but all the noblemen are also free, released by their "nobler reason" from their "furie." The lesson has been taught; the master lays aside his staff and book; solemnity is forgotten, as all—master and students alike—return to the world of bees, cowslips, and owls.

The Music and Its Performance

As a starting point in reconstructing the original performance of the music in *The Tempest,* we should know as much as possible about the physical conditions surrounding the first productions of the play.[5] Little is known about the production in 1611 except that it was produced in the Whitehall Banqueting House. Some evidence will here be presented that the production of 1613 also occurred in the Banqueting House at Whitehall, a structure designed primarily for the presentation of the great Stuart masques. If we consider the 1613 production of the play at Whitehall as a reasonable hypothesis, what sort of stage would have been available to Shakespeare?

According to Nicoll, *Stuart Masques and the Renaissance Stage,* pp. 32-53, the Banqueting House in general structure must have resembled the plan drawn by Inigo Jones for *Florimène.* By the time this latter entertainment was projected, the Banqueting House of 1613 had burned; but its successor, for which Jones' plan was drawn, was built on the foundations of the original building and therefore probably preserved the dimensions of the original.[6] This plan shows a rectangular auditorium. At one end and against the sides of the auditorium are boxes or tiers of seats rising from the floor. Within this U of seats, the "state," or separate platform-throne of the king and his intimates, is placed in the center of the floor. At the opposite end of the hall is a stage, actually a temporary structure whose floor is raised about six feet above the auditorium floor. Between the state and the stage is a "dancing place" connected with the stage by a ramp or stairway. Also on the floor level of the auditorium Jones' plan shows a box for musicians. This box is placed against the left wall, as one faces the stage, where it is close to the dancing place and also adjoins the left corner of the stage. This is a practical location, as it permits the music made there to serve both the action on the stage and the dancers who perform in the area between the stage and the state. However, as accounts of the Whitehall masques produced in 1613 indicate, the musicians were also placed in other areas of the dancing place and the stage.

Since the stages varied in construction from time to time, the form used for *The Tempest* can best be determined by a study of the descriptions of three masques produced for the same occasion as Shakespeare's play. These masques were Campion's *Lords Masque,* produced February 14, 1613; Chapman's *Masque of the Middle Temple and Lincoln's Inn,* on the following evening; and Beaumont's *Masque of the Inner Temple and Gray's Inn,* on February 20.[7] Two halls of Whitehall served for these performances—the "banqueting house" or "masking hall," and a smaller room, the "great hall." Chapman's masque was given in the "great hall," probably, as Chambers suggests, because the "banqueting house" still contained the stage and scenery of Campion's masque presented the preceding night.[8] Beaumont's masque was apparently presented in the banqueting house.[9] Withal, to judge from the descriptions of the three masques, the stages on which they were presented were quite similar; any one could have served to mount *The Tempest.*

The most prominent feature common to the three stages was a horizontal division into two levels. The upper stage was set slightly back from the front of the lower stage. Campion describes this in his account of *The Lord's Masque.* The upper stage portrayed either the heavens or the tops of high mountains. The lower stage showed caves, woods, gardens, or seascapes. Campion describes his complete stage as follows (Campion, *Campion's Works,* pp. 89, 92):

The Scene *was divided into two parts from the roofe to the floore, the lower part being first discovered (upon the sound of a double consort, expresst by severall instruments, plac't on either side of the roome) there appeared a Wood in prospective, the innermost part being of releave or whole round, the rest painted. On the left hand from the seate* [*state?*] *was a Cave, and on the right a thicket . . . the Upper part of the Scene was discovered by the sodaine fall of a curtaine; then in clowdes of severall colours . . . appeared eight Starres of extraordinarie bignesse, which were so placed, as that they seemed to be fixed betweene the Firmament and the Earth. . . .*

The first scene of the *Middle Temple Masque* showed

. . . an Artificiall Rock, whose top was neer as high as the Hall it selfe. This Rock was in the undermost part craggy and full of hollow places, in whose concaves were contriv'd two winding paire of staires by whose greeces the Persons above might make their descents and all the way be seene. . . . On the other side of the Rocke grewe a Grove, in whose utmost part appear'd a vast, wither'd and hollow Tree, being the bare receptacle of the Baboonerie . . . the upper part of the rock was sodainly turn'd to a Cloude, discovering a rich and refulgent Mine of golde . . . (Chapman, *The Memorable Masque,* B4, B5).

The *Masque of the Inner Temple* showed a similar scene.

Here also 'the Fabricke was a Mountaine with two descents,' covered by a pair of curtains; evidently a combination was being made of the horizontally divided stage of *Lords* and the practicable rock set of Chapman's masque. . . . 'The first Travers was drawne . . . and the lower descent of the Mountaine discovered, which was the Pendant of a hill to life, with divers boscages and Grovets upon the steepe or hanging grounds thereof; . . .' The second traverse was drawn, 'and the higher ascent of the Mountaine is discovered,' . . . (Nicoll, *op. cit.,* pp. 33, 34).

It thus appears that the stages available at Whitehall for *The Tempest* each consisted of three "scenes." One was the dancing place, or bare area, between the state and the stage structure. This would correspond to the "platea" of the early stages. From this area a ramp or stairs led up to the middle "scene" or stage proper about six feet above the dancing place.[10] The upper "scene" was joined to the lower by a gradually ascending stairway. The middle scene contained a "rock" or mountain in which could have been a cave at the left side. At the right side of the middle scene would have been a grove of woods, in the center a forest or sea "prospective."[11] The upper scene showed the top of the rock or mountain and various cloud or astral effects. The musicians could have been placed on either side of the dancing place or at many possible points on the upper and middle scenes.

While we are concerned with the stage facilities of the early productions of the play, we should also inquire as to the musical establishment available for Shakespeare's use. The players may have brought their own consort to court with them, but this would be carrying coals to Newcastle. Rather, the quantity of music and dance in the play suggests that musicians and dancers from the court may have been used. No doubt the quality of the dancing and music was higher than the usual theater personnel could provide. If the same stage and scenery were used for the play as were used for the three masques performed on the same occasion, why should not some of the musicians and dancers who performed in the masques be used for the play? Let us see what music was used in the masques.

Campion's account of the *Lords' Masque* mentions a "double consort," placed on both sides of the hall, which apparently means in front of the middle scene and on each side of the dancing place. He also speaks of twelve dancers who perform an anti-mask "Lunatickes" dance. The vocal music was primarily choral; Campion mentions "Full songs," and "Chorus"; however, a dialogue song and perhaps one or two solo songs were also presented. The location of the singers is not clear. The only reference to them is when Orpheus exclaims, "Flie, cheerfull voices, through the ayre, and clear/ These clouds, that yon hid beautie may appeare."

In Beaumont's *Inner Temple Masque* after a dance of Cupids "the music changed from violins to hautboys, cornets &c.," and later we see Jupiter's Priests, "every Priest playing upon a lute; twelve in number." The priests also sing. Later on "loud music sounds. . . . "

The masque also presents an anti-mask of rustic dancers (Evans, *English Masques,* pp. 94-98).

The account of Chapman's *Middle Temple Masque* reports "choice musicians of our kingdom, six in each [car], attired like Virginian priests" who journeyed with the masquers to Whitehall. These twelve musicians included, apparently, six lutenists and six vocalists who played and sang during the masque. "Other music and voices," perhaps from the court musical establishment, are mentioned as taking part in the performance (Chapman, *op cit.*).

While we might not expect Shakespeare's play to be as lavishly supported as were the masques, we may suspect that some of these dancers and musicians joined forces with the King's Men for their royal performance. Certainly some sort of collaboration between the masque musicians and the players is indicated by the fact that one of the principal composers who supplied music for two of the masques is also generally credited with the composition of musical settings for two songs in the play.

Several musicians and composers pooled their efforts in composing the music for one or more of the three masques. Among them were Thomas Campion, John Coperario (Cooper), Philip Rossiter, Robert Johnson, Thomas Ford, John and Robert Dowland, Thomas Lupo the Elder, and Alexander Chisan.[12] Any of this galaxy could have worked with the players, but we are reasonably sure that one did. Robert Johnson is believed by most scholars to have composed the music to "Full Fathom Five" and "Where the Bee Sucks" for the revival of the play in 1613. It is also quite probable that he composed the music, now lost, for "Come unto these yellow sands"[13] and for the masque song of Juno and Ceres.

It thus seems safe to assume that an unusually excellent musical group was available for use with the King's Men. Johnson's collaboration with the company in its production of *The Tempest* is some evidence that lesser instrumentalists and dancers may have been likewise employed.

With some consideration of the stage and musical facilities at hand, we may now attempt a reconstruction of the musical episodes as performed at the Court in 1613.

The initial incident (I, ii) presents Ariel singing in order to draw Ferdinand from the edge of the sea into the presence of Prospero and Miranda. The stage direction is *Enter Ferdinand & Ariel, invisible playing & singing.* Suppose we now place the actors on the stage and reconstruct the action. Prospero and Miranda are seated in front of the cave at the left side of the middle scene, as viewed by the audience. Ferdinand walks onto the dancing place in front of and below the middle scene. But where is Ariel? The stage direction is ambiguous. Does Ariel enter with Ferdinand, invisible to Ferdinand only? Or is Ariel invisible to both Ferdinand and audience? Obviously Ferdinand cannot determine the origin of the music played by Ariel. He exclaims, "Where shold this Musick be? I'th aire, or th' earth?" Also, Ariel addresses his song to the "sweete Sprights." It does not seem likely that if he is visible to the audience, he should be addressing spirits like himself but who are not visible. Rather it seems that the spectacular element of the play would be better served by the visible dancing and singing of Ariel and his sprites around Ferdinand. And dramatic logic places Ariel and the dancers in the dancing place between the raised stage and the royal state. Ariel, who we assume is a singing boy, sings the song and plays his own accompaniment on a lute.[14] In the great hall some instrumental support of the relatively feeble music of the lute is necessary. After a solo passage ending with " . . . sweete Sprights the burthen beare,"[15] other voices join Ariel, apparently from scattered points about the scenes.

In the absence of the original score for this song it is difficult to determine how the parts were divided. The problem is further complicated by the apparent textual corruption of the burden and Ariel's final lines. The meter of Ariel's first six lines is quite regular, but thereafter no regularity is noticeable. We can only guess that following the solo part the air is filled with various animal cries sung in such a way as to echo from several sides of the playing area and to form a repetitious underpart above which Ariel sings the final portion of the song.

For practical purposes the concluding portion of the text has been regularized and the resulting complete version set to a popular ayre by John Dowland (Fig. 34). This ayre appears in a contemporary manuscript of lute tablature (Folger Shakespeare Library MS 1610.1) with the title "The Frog Galliard." Under this title it is also scored for broken consort in Morley's *First Booke of Consort*

FIGURE 34.—Come unto these yellow sands

Lessons (1599 and 1611). Dowland also used the music as a setting for his song "Now O now I needs must part." The same melody, usually credited to Dowland, is found in many lute and song collections of the early seventeenth century, both in England and on the Continent.

Scansion of the lyric of "Come unto these yellow sands" suggests that the song was an ayre quite possibly set by Robert Johnson, as its form and performance are closely related to "Full Fathom Five" by Johnson, which follows almost immediately. This poignant little elegy was apparently performed in the same manner as the first song. Ariel sings the first several lines solo. Upon Ariel's completion of the line *Into something rich, & strange,* the same echoing voices, only this time coming from the sea-nymphs, intone the repeated "ding dong" which form the burden to the final line, *Harke now I heare them, ding-dong bell.* Both songs are thus parts of one dramatic effect. The first welcomes Ferdinand to the island and to human society; the second is a consoling farewell from the sea spirits which, as Ferdinand remarks, "do's remember my drown'd father," and which also prefigures Ferdinand's comment in the final act of the play, "Though the Seas threaten they are mercifull./ I have curs'd them without cause."

The earliest setting of "Full Fathom Five" is printed in John Wilson's *Cheerfull Ayres or Ballads* (1660); the setting is reproduced in the Appendix. An arrangement of the song as it could have been performed according to our reconstruction is shown in Figure 35.

But to return to the stage. Between the performance of the two songs Ferdinand begins to walk from the dancing place toward the incline leading up to the middle scene where Prospero and Miranda sit in front of the cave. At the conclusion of the elegy Ferdinand is near the middle scene, perhaps at the foot of the incline. The music which draws him toward Miranda does not cease with the ending of the sea-nymphs' song; it is continued by a consort of instruments placed probably behind the scenery of the upper scene. Ferdinand indicates the shift in origin of the music when he exclaims, "This is no mortall busines, nor no sound/ That the earth owes: I heare it now above me." The "it" refers to the music of the ditty sung by Ariel. The consort picks up the music of "Full Fathom Five" and plays it softly while Ferdinand walks up the incline to the lower stage (middle scene) and addresses Miranda. The music

Full fathom five thy fa - ther lies; Of his bones are coral made; Those are
pearls that were his eyes; Nothing of him that doth fade, But doth suffer a sea-change
Into something rich and strange. Sea-nymphs hour-ly ring his knell: Hark! now I
hear them, Hark, now I hear them, Ding - dong bell.

FIGURE 35.—Full fadom five

for this romantic moment is supplied by a consort of viols or recorders. The music is necessarily soft, as Prospero and Miranda, and possibly Ferdinand, speak several lines above the music.

The music by which Ariel puts Alonso and Gonzalo to sleep in II, i, is evidently performed by Ariel alone. The stage direction states, *Enter Ariell playing solemne Musicke.* The instrument most appropriate for solemn music here is the tenor recorder, whose mellow, woody music is both solemn and sleep-inducing. An excellent musical score for this episode is "The Duchesse of Brunswick's Toye" by John Bull. This melody taken from the Fitzwilliam Virginal Book is given in Figure 36.[16]

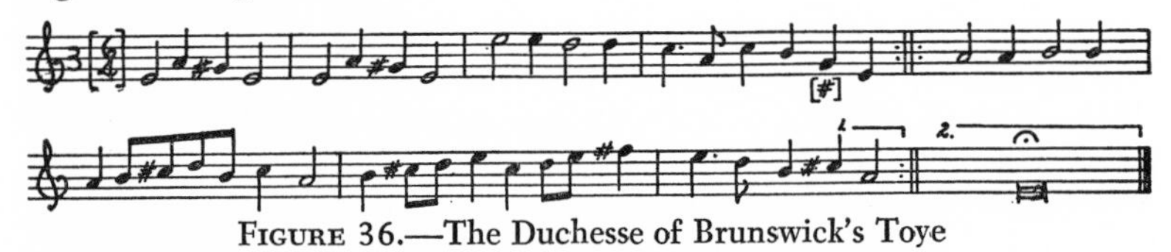

FIGURE 36.—The Duchesse of Brunswick's Toye

The logical place for the enactment of this episode is the lower scene which throughout the play represents any part of the island other than the location of Prospero's cell. Ariel enters upon his cue; he is of course invisible to the royal party, though, in the absence of evidence to the contrary, seen by the audience. At some point after all members of the party except Antonio and Sebastian have fallen asleep, Ariel leaves the scene. The two conspirators form their plot to murder the King.

Just as Antonio raises his sword (possibly the cue for Ariel and the musicians, if any supported him),[17] Ariel appears and sings his warning "While you here do snoaring lie" in Gonzalo's ear. The stage direction is *Enter Ariell with Musicke and Song.* This suggests that Ariel does not play music here, but rather sings to an instrumental accompaniment provided by a consort. Certainly it would be awkward for Ariel to play any form of lute or viol and to try to sing near the ear of the recumbent Gonzalo at the same time.

Since the original music is missing, the song is here set to the music of a "hunts-up" or awakening song by John Bennet as found in T. Ravenscroft's *Briefe Discourse* . . . (1614). Our setting is shown in Figure 37.

FIGURE 37.—While you here do snoaring lie

In the following scene (II, ii), Caliban appears in the dancing place closely followed by Trinculo. Stephano then reels into the scene happily and drunkenly bellowing a sea chantey, *I shall no more to sea, to sea, here shall I dye ashore.* He is displeased with his first burst of song and begins on another tack, *The Master, the Swabber, the Boate-swaine & I.* Stephano sings without accompaniment; the text mentions no musical instrument, and Stephano's bottle would keep his hands occupied. The sea chantey, one of the earliest known in English, is a folk-type song that requires little or no musical training for its performance.[18] Stephano himself refers to his rendition as a "scurvy tune." His voice and musicianship need only have been barely sufficient for him to carry a tune in a ludicrous manner.

The tune to which the chantey was sung or bellowed is not known, not surprising in this case, as it was probably set to some ballad tune. By what may be more than a fortunate coincidence, however, the tune of an old song called "The Leather Bottél" fits almost exactly the text of the song. The tune dates from the time of Queen Mary or possibly earlier.[19]

"The Leather Bottél" is a drinking song, which makes it appropriate for Stephano's use at this time, but a scurvy tune to sing at a man's funeral. The text of Stephano's chantey fits the tune

FIGURE 38.—The Leather Bottél

almost exactly; the turn in the thought of both songs occurs at the break in measure 8 (Figs. 38 and 39); the climax of both songs falls in measure 16, which in the case of the chantey contains the anatomical reference most likely to be appreciated and therefore sung more lustily by a sailor. If Shakespeare did not write or borrow the chantey with the tune of "The Leather Bottél" in mind, he overlooked a most appropriate musical setting.

Caliban makes his first bow as a musician in the same scene (line 182), when he sings his drunken praise of what he thinks is freedom.

Caliban Sings drunkenly.

Farewell Master; farewell, farewell.
Tri. A howling Monster: a drunken Monster.
Cal. No more dams I'le make for fish, etc.

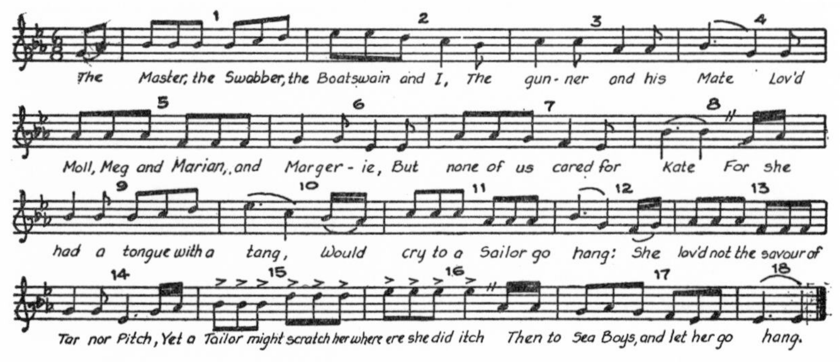

FIGURE 39.—The Master, the Swabber, the Boate-swain & I

The imagination is staggered by an attempt to re-create Caliban's vocal effects. Just how would such a monster sing, particularly when in his cups? Certainly the quality of his music would be very poor. Perhaps he did not really sing, but, as Trinculo remarks, howled his song. The First Folio text separates the line "Farewell Master; farewell, farewell" from the song proper. Several editors suggest that this line should follow Trinculo's descriptive line rather than precede it.[20] But we may disagree with them: it seems that Trinculo should hear Caliban's attempt at music before he comments on the quality of the music. Yet the line is probably a part of the song: most folk-type songs, of which Caliban's seems to be a sect or scion, usually have an even number of lines, and the line in question is necessary for an even quantity. As for the tune of Caliban's song, we shall make no effort here to supply what is best left to the imagination.

In III, ii, the befuddled conspirators attempt a more complex form of music; they try to sing a catch together. Apparently Stephano and Trinculo have given Caliban a music lesson in a futile attempt to improve his skill. Caliban asks, "Will you troule the Catch/ You taught me but whileare?" The catch is one of the most simple forms of part-song, but even so the three rascals cannot manage it. Ariel, invisible to the three, has to correct them by playing the tune on his pipe and tabor. While he plays the Pied Piper, he leads the rats off the scene. The catch for three voices shown in Figure 40 seems fitting for a pipe and tabor, and the text is especially applicable to our three sots. This catch was written by John Hilton probably in the first half of the seventeenth century. The version shown in Figure 40 is a transcription of the catch as printed in John Playford's *Catch that Catch Can* (1673), p. 34.

In the next scene (III, iii) the party of noblemen moves back

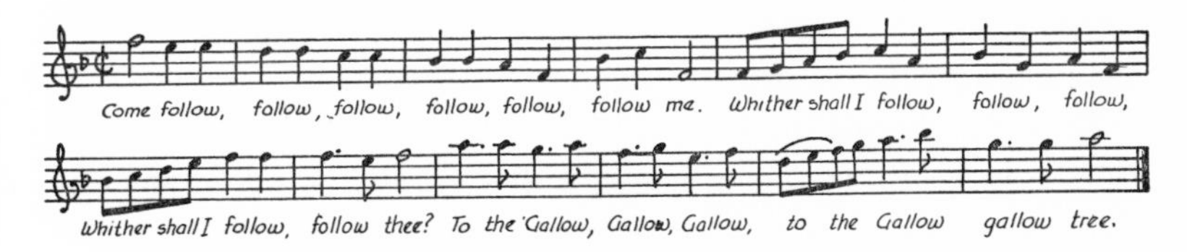

FIGURE 40.—Come follow, follow

into the dancing place. The weary and despondent men are confronted by Ariel's shapes who bring before them a table covered with tempting food.

The staging of this episode must have been fairly elaborate, though perhaps not as complicated as that suggested by J. C. Adams.[21] The atmosphere of the magical banquet is set by the consort's *Solemne and strange Musicke* to which the shapes bring in a table spread with dishes. This method of stage setting would have been necessary for the lower scene which, being the permanent floor of the hall, had no trap doors. The music evokes the quality of magic and also fulfills its conventional function at similar normal festivities. It invites the participants to good cheer and fellowship, to a harmonious gathering.

The consort supplying the music was probably hidden behind the mountain top on the upper (celestial) scene. Here also is where Prospero stands, not only for the symbolic effect achieved, but also to coordinate the activities of the musicians and dancers, neither of whom could probably have seen the other. The pavane with its stately, processional steps seems the likely form of music for the entering and departing dances of the strange servitors. Provided for use here is a pavane or "masque" with the title "The Tempest" (Fig. 41). This is possibly the piece of music from the 1613 production which Francis Rimbault claimed to have recovered, although he did not say where it was found. Both he and John Cutts, who recently re-recovered the music, attribute it to Robert Johnson.[22] The title of the piece and its location among other theatrical music in the manuscript, much of it by Robert Johnson, convince Cutts that both "The Tempest" and an accompanying "Masque" were written by Johnson for Shakespeare's play. Both compositions may be found in British Museum Add. MS 10444 (see Appendix). A modern transcription of "The Tempest" has been published in the Arden edition of *The Tempest* (1954), edited by Frank Kermode.

The center of the action now moves to the middle scene in front of Prospero's cell (IV, i). In honor of the betrothal of Ferdinand and Miranda (and of course the real Prince Frederick and Princess Elizabeth) he promises to "Bestow upon the eyes of this young couple/

Some vanity of mine Art." Ariel is dispatched to bring in the spirits who will present the masque. Then, *Soft musick. Enter Iris.*

This music, probably from the consort of viols or recorders hidden behind the mountain, is fitting for the appearance of the rainbow goddess, the messenger of the goddesses; and it also provides a dramatic contrast to the thunder which marked the appearance of the avenging harpy in the previous "show." Against this soft music Iris delivers her summons, with its lovely nature poetry, to Ceres. Before she is through with her evocation, she gives the cue, line 70, for Juno to begin her descent. Ceres then enters, to whom Iris explains that Venus and Cupid have failed to interfere with the sanctity of the marriage vows proclaimed by the betrothed couple (historical and

FIGURE 41.—The Tempest

dramatic) and that Juno is to join the Olympians in blessing the betrothal.

While this mixture of poetry and music is carried on, Juno appears from behind the mountain-top on the upper scene and slowly descends by a ramp or stairway to the middle scene.[23] There she joins Iris and Ceres; the latter probably entered from the "woods" opposite the cave or cell.

The quality of the poetry, the divine speakers, and the dignity of the occasion suggest that the *Soft musick* is gentle and lyrical in quality. The text also gives an indication that perhaps only two of the three immortals sing. Iris, perhaps because she is an inferior of the other two, does not sing with them. Juno sings the first four lines, then Ceres takes her turn and completes the remaining eight lines. Thus, the two do not sing together; Juno and Ceres actually sing their parts in sequence.

The vocalists who took these parts were probably two singing boys or rather, to be accurate, Ariel and an additional singing boy. As Dover Wilson has noted, Ariel doubles as Ceres.[24] Ariel later tells Prospero, "I my Commander, when I presented Ceres/ I thought to have told thee of it, but I fear'd/ Lest I might anger thee." The subject of the song and the divine nature of its singers make an art-song, or ayre, almost the requisite type of setting, and probably one played by the same consort that introduced Iris. In Figure 42 the nuptial hymn of Juno and Ceres is set to what seems to be a masque song by William Lawes, as it appears in the New York Public Library

FIGURE 42.—Honor, riches, marriage, blessing

MS Drexel 4257. A guess would place the date of Lawes' song somewhere between 1625 and 1650. The fit of Shakespeare's song text with Lawes' music (see Appendix) is surprisingly close, perhaps because both lyrics employ a simple, though rather unusual, trochaic meter.

Juno and Ceres send Iris away. She returns with a group of nymphs and another group of reapers, who join in a dance. This pastoral dance, it seems, is not the usual country dance such as the morris or the hay, which are not usually marked by the finest grace in movements. The dancers in this case are twice-removed from actual countryfolk. A courtly dance form as the galliard (derived from a folk-dance) seems more suitable for the occasion. For the same reason the dance music, supposedly ethereal in origin, is supplied by a consort rather than by the tabor and pipe, crowd, or bagpipe, the instruments usually associated with rural music. The treble viol part of a pleasant gallaird may be seen in Figure 43. It is titled "Galliard to Phillips Pavin" and is No. 9 in Morley's *First Booke of Consort Lessons* (1599).

The dancers then "heavily vanish," presumably through a trap door in the floor of the middle scene where the dancers performed before Ferdinand and Miranda.[25] The "hollow and confused noyse" could have been made by the machinery under the stage floor; but it also may have been some type of music used to cover the noise of the machinery. In the masque *Tempe Restored* among the performers on the stage were children "riding on tame beasts and some blowing such wrethen Trumps as make confused noyse."[26]

The climax of the play is reached when Prospero, having achiev-

FIGURE 43.—Galliard to Phillips Pavin

ed his beneficent end, renounces his magic. The "heavenly Musicke" required by Prospero at this point appropriately would be sounded by the consort hidden behind the mountain peak. The music begins at Prospero's cue. As the music is used to cure the brains of the enchanted noblemen, it probably continues to sound while "Their understanding/ Begins to swell," that is, until Prospero sends Ariel to fetch his hat and rapier. Arbeau's *Orchesography* (1588) furnishes us with a "Pavan," shown in Figure 44, which has a gravity and suggestion of mystery fitting for this episode.

Ariell sings, and helps to attire him. He sings, of course, to cover the awkward pause in the action while Prospero removes his magical robe and, visually, assumes his former place in the world of men. But the song (see Robert Johnson's setting in Figure 45 and the Appendix) also changes the whole tone of the play from solemnity and mystery to joy in well-earned liberty. To the strains of the consort and the singing of the blithe spirit, schoolmaster and pupils alike lift their eyes from the allegorical textbook to the sensible world of government and cities, bats and blossoms, which now appears brave and new since all have found themselves "When no man was his owne." With Ariel's happy caroling the music of the isle fades away, leaving in its place "calme Seas, auspicious gales,/ And saile so expeditious, that shall catch/Your Royall fleet farre off. . . ."

FIGURE 44.—Pavan

FIGURE 45.—Where the Bee Sucks

Notes

1. *William Shakespeare,* I, 491, and II, 342, 343.
2. Prof. W. C. Curry *(Shakespeare's Philosophical Patterns)* is inclined to discount allegorical interpretations of the play which he believes should be understood literally. His caveat, however, does not seem to be directed at the

analogical explanation presented here, which is well within the province of the medieval accommodations inherited by the Renaissance world.
3. All quotations from the play are from the First Folio text unless otherwise noted. Line numbers follow the Globe edition.
4. Noble, *Shakespeare's Use of Song,* p. 107.
5. The Following reconstruction of the staging of *The Tempest* in 1613 was made before I was able to obtain a copy of Ernest Law's "Shakespeare's 'Tempest' as Originally Produced at Court." Nor had I consulted J. Isaacs' "Production and Stage Management at the Blackfriars Theatre" or L. B. Campbell's *Scenes and Machines on the English Stage during the Renaissance.* All these students place the production of the play at Blackfriars, though with varying degrees of conviction. Frank Kermode, editor of the Arden edition (Appendix E, "*The Tempest* on the Jacobean Stage," pp. 150-155) notes the "quite certain" performance at the Banqueting House at Whitehall in 1611 and believes that performances could have occurred at the Globe or the permanent Banqueting House or at Blackfriars Theatre between 1611 and 1613, "But the Blackfriars was the natural home of the play." Most of this authoritative opinion rests, ultimately, on Dryden's comment in his Preface to *The Tempest or the Enchanted Island* (1670): " . . . the play itself had formerly been acted with success in the Black-Fryers." This remark does not deny the possibility of performances elsewhere.
6. *Florimène* was produced in 1633. Nicoll doubts that there were any significant changes in the structure of the masquing hall in the intervening time.
7. For contemporary accounts of these masques see G. Chapman, *The Memorable Masque . . .* (1613); F. Beaumont, *The Masque of the Inner Temple . . .* (1613); T. Campion, *Campion's Works;* Evans, *English Masques;* and Chapman, *The Plays and Poems of George Chapman,* II.
8. Concerning these two halls see Chambers, *The Elizabethan Stage,* I, 202, 225, 226, and Nicoll, *Stuart Masques and the Renaissance Stage,* pp. 32-38.
9. Nicoll, *op. cit.,* pp. 33, 34.
10. C. Hodges *(The Globe Restored,* pp. 34-50) describes several scaffold stages of the period as being about six feet high.
11. For an account of the symbolic functions of these units of setting see G. Kernodle, *From Art to Theatre,* pp. 72-108.
12. Chambers, *op. cit.,* I, 202.
13. Compare the structures and methods of performance of the first two songs in the play.
14. Noble *(op. cit.)* believes Ariel was acted by a young man.
15. This line quoted as amended by Theobald.
16. Fitzwilliam Virginal Book, II, No. 9.
17. As noted by J. Adams, *The Globe Playhouse,* p. 315.
18. Noble, *op. cit.,* p. 16, Fn. 2. F. Kermode (Arden edition [1954], p. 63, Fn. 43) does not believe this is an actual chantey "as the lines have not the marks of the working-song. The second song is also too sophisticated." But note how easily the lines fit a drinking-song tune and how easily this tune with its strong rhythmic beat may be used for a working-song.
19. Gibbon, *Melody and the Lyric,* p. 44.
20. For example, Luce, Arden edition, p. 77, Fn. 190.
21. "The Staging of 'The Tempest,' III, iii," pp. 404 ff.
22. Cutts, "Robert Johnson: King's Musician . . . ," pp. 110-125.

23. Lawrence ("The Masque in the Tempest," p. 943) believes that Juno walked onto the stage but is puzzled by her "double entry." Collier (quoted by Kittredge) thinks that she was lowered by some machine. Kittredge thinks line 71 too early for Juno to appear, and that she is not seen until line 100, when she appears walking (*The Tempest,* p. 134). But Juno could appear at the mountain top at line 70, walk down an incline, and reach the floor of the middle scene about line 100. Kermode (Arden edition, p. 97, Fn. 72) suggests that Juno starts her passage to earth at about line 70.
24. Noble, "Shakespeare's Songs and Stage," p. 133.
25. Nicoll, *op. cit.,* pp. 38, 58.
26. *Ibid.,* p. 47.

EIGHT

Conclusion

HEN WE REFLECT UPON SHAKESPEARE'S USE OF music in the final comedies, it becomes apparent that he used music most frequently for three purposes: to underscore climactic or crucial scenes, to make the supernatural perceptible, and to symbolize abstract or psychological ideas. These three effects are usually interrelated and in many instances are achieved simultaneously in performance. The point at which they converge is the theme around which the last four comedies—*Pericles, Cymbeline, The Winter's Tale,* and *The Tempest*—are constructed, that is, the recognition by a dramatic character of a transcendent Truth concerning divine providence. When we also remember that throughout the final comedies a revival of Shakespeare's dramatic and poetic creativity is closely paralleled by an increase in the quantity and effectiveness of the music he uses, we are provided with much food for thought on the relationship of music not only to Shakespeare's creative power but also to the poetry in general.

The climactic scene in *Pericles,* discernible in spite of the loosely-constructed plot, is the recognition of Marina by Pericles and his perception of divine intercession as revealed by the music of the spheres. Here the music increases the emotional impact of the scene on the audience, supplies the supernatural voice of the gods, which, in turn, assures Pericles of the benign providence that will subsequently complete the reunion of his family. Likewise, in *Cymbeline* the music of the masque is a part of the ritual in which Jupiter is importuned by the ghosts of Posthumus' family. The god appears and leaves with the sleeping Posthumus the golden tablet that will resolve all his difficulties. Jupiter explains his providence as he addresses his ghostly suppliants: "Be not with mortall accidents opprest,/ No care of yours it is, you know 'tis ours./ Whom best I love, I crosse; to make my guift/ The more delay'd, delighted."

The result is that Cymbeline is reunited with his family, Posthumus is reunited with Imogen, Iachimo is pardoned, and Rome and Britain reconciled. As the Soothsayer states, "The fingers of the Powres above, do tune/ The harmony of this Peace. . . . " The masque scene is thus the turning point of the action and a statement of the theme of the play. Music, both in performance and imagery, brings the scene to a focus.

In *The Winter's Tale,* likewise, the climax of the play occurs with the reunion of Leontes, Perdita, and Hermione just after Hermione has been revived by music. It is she who states the theme of providence. "You Gods looke downe,/ And from your sacred Viols poure your graces/ Upon my daughters head: . . . For thou [Perdita] shalt heare that I/ Knowing by *Paulina,* that the Oracle/ Gave hope thou wast in being, have preserv'd/ My selfe, to see the yssue."

The climax of *The Tempest* is Prospero's renunciation of magic and the simultaneous restoration of the noblemen to a harmonious relationship—all done to the sound of "heavenly Musicke." After the establishment of individual, political, social, and familial harmony, Ferdinand speaks the theme of providence. "Though the Seas threaten they are mercifull,/ I have curs'd them without cause."

The association of music with the idea of Harmony, in the sense of the individual's relationship with himself, with his family, with the state, and with the natural and supernatural worlds, the relationships between social classes and between nations, reveals a broad, though not systematic, philosophy. This philosophy, consciously or subconsciously, underlies Shakespeare's use of music both in actual performance and, we may suspect, in imagery.

It is not difficult to determine the mainstream of the philosophy he follows. The association of harmony or music with human relationships is a prominent concept of the Renaissance derived from Platonic thought. One of the great themes of Plato's *Republic* is, we remember, Socrates' definition of Justice as Harmony—in the individual, a harmonious functioning of the three elements, reason, passion, concupiscence; in the state, the concordant operation of the guardians, the auxiliaries, and husbandmen. Therein also appears the hypothesis that the kind of music a people choose will determine the quality of the laws they will make.

There can be little doubt that the rather amorphous Neo-Platonism set forth by Ficino, Agrippa, and Fludd, to name only a few, as well as by Mersenne and Barnes, provided Shakespeare with many of the concepts that seem to control his use of music, particularly in the last four plays covered by this study. The consistency with which the concepts appear suggests that they are not expedient dramatic devices alone but a part of the permanent furniture of Shakespeare's mind. If this be true, then we have gained an additional insight that should enable us to understand better the poet and the man.

The parallel increase in the quantity and quality of the music used in the later comedies and the increase in the poetic, dramatic, and philosophical power of Shakespeare provide us with a fairly definite statement on the relationship of music and poetry. *The Taming of the Shrew* and *The Merry Wives of Windsor* are primarily farces: *Measure for Measure* and *All's Well That Ends Well* probe the depths of human frailty, but Shakespeare's hand is uncertain and sometimes falters. It is only in the last four comedies that the theme of divine providence and human harmony becomes clearly defined, and with this definition occurs a resurgence of creative power.

Granted that external factors, such as the influences of the court masques and court tastes, may have had some effect on Shakespeare's employment of music in these comedies, the weight of evidence supports the belief that the association of poetry and music was a part of one inner process. When Shakespeare rides the crest of a great wave of feeling, he rises to transcendent heights by means of poetry, symbolism, and music—three successive steps of an escape from the limitations of language toward a universal expression of that Platonic Harmony which even the monster, Caliban, could discern and which could move him to utter in beautiful simplicity the lines which close this study:

Be not affeard, the Isle is full of noyses,
Sounds, and sweet aires, that give delight and hurt not:
Sometimes a thousand twangling Instruments
Will hum about mine eares; and sometimes voices,
That if I then had wak'd after long sleepe,
Will make me sleepe againe, and then in dreaming,
The clouds methought would open, and shew riches
Ready to drop upon me, that when I wak'd
I cri'de to dreame againe.

Appendix

HE FOLLOWING PHOTOGRAPHIC REPRODUCTIONS of musical documents are here presented because of their value to the musicologist and to the serious student of Shakespeare. These few examples do not exhaust the available body of early musical settings associated in one way or another with Shakespeare; most of the selections were chosen because they are the earliest known settings; others are included because they have not been previously published, though they are not necessarily the earliest settings.

"Take o take those lips away." This setting by John Wilson appears, with slight variations, in several sources. While this is probably not the earliest version of Wilson's setting, it has not been previously published, as far as I know. *Source:* New York Public Library MS Drexel 4041.

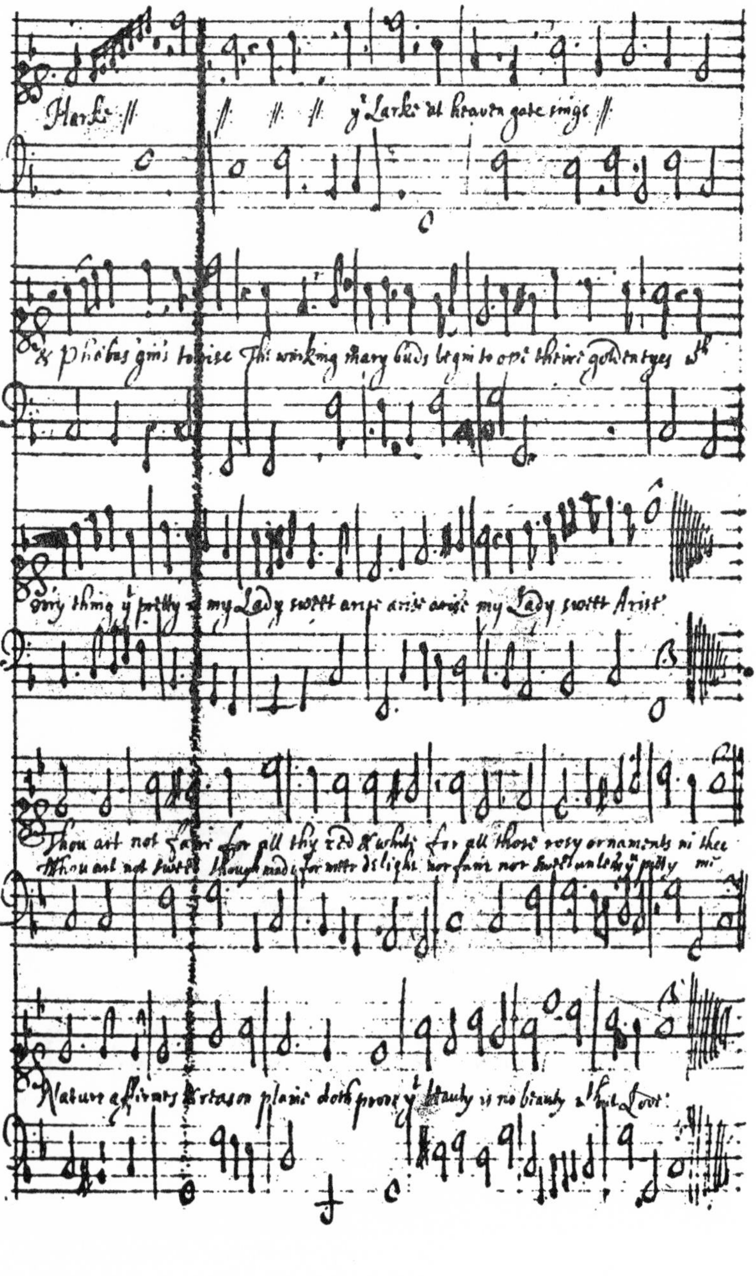
Hark
y Larke at heaven gate sings
& Phebus gin's to rise The winking mary buds begin to ope theire golden eyes with
every thing y pritty is my Lady sweete arise arise arise my Lady sweete Arise
Thou art not faire for all thy red & white for all those rosy ornaments in thee
Thou art not sweete though made for mere delight nor faire nor sweet unless thou pitty me
Nature affirms & reason plaine doth prove y beauty is no beauty without Love

a. 3. Voc.
[85]
Mr. John Hilton.
Og on, Jog on the Foot-path way, and mer-ri-ly hent the Stile-a, the
Merry heart goes all day long, the Sad tyres in a Mile-a : Your paltry
Money Bags of Gold, what need have we to ſtare for, when little or nothing ſoon
is told, and we have the leſs to care for : Caſt care away, care away, let ſorrow
ceaſe, a fig for Melancho-ly, let's laugh and ſing, laugh and ſing, or if you pleaſe,
wee'l frolick with ſweet Molly. Jog on, &c.

"Jog on, Jog on." The well-known setting by John Hilton. *Source:* John Playford. *The Musical Companion* (1673).

FACING

"Harke, harke, ye Larke." An incomplete setting previously published, most recently by Professor Peter Seng. *Source:* Bodleian Library MS Don. c. 57.

GET YOU HENCE FOR I MUST GOE

Get you hence, for I must goe." This setting has been recently published for the first time by Professor John Cutts. It was found in a MS formerly owned by Francis Rimbault and afterwards by J. Stafford Smith. Apparently neither of these students of early English music discovered the song. *Source:* New York Public Library MS Drexel 4175, "Songs unto the Violl and Lute" (c. 1620).

THE SATYRE'S MASQUE

"The Satyres Masque." Professor John Cutts suggests that this is the music used for the dance of the Satyrs in *The Winter's Tale. Source:* British Museum Add. MS 10444.

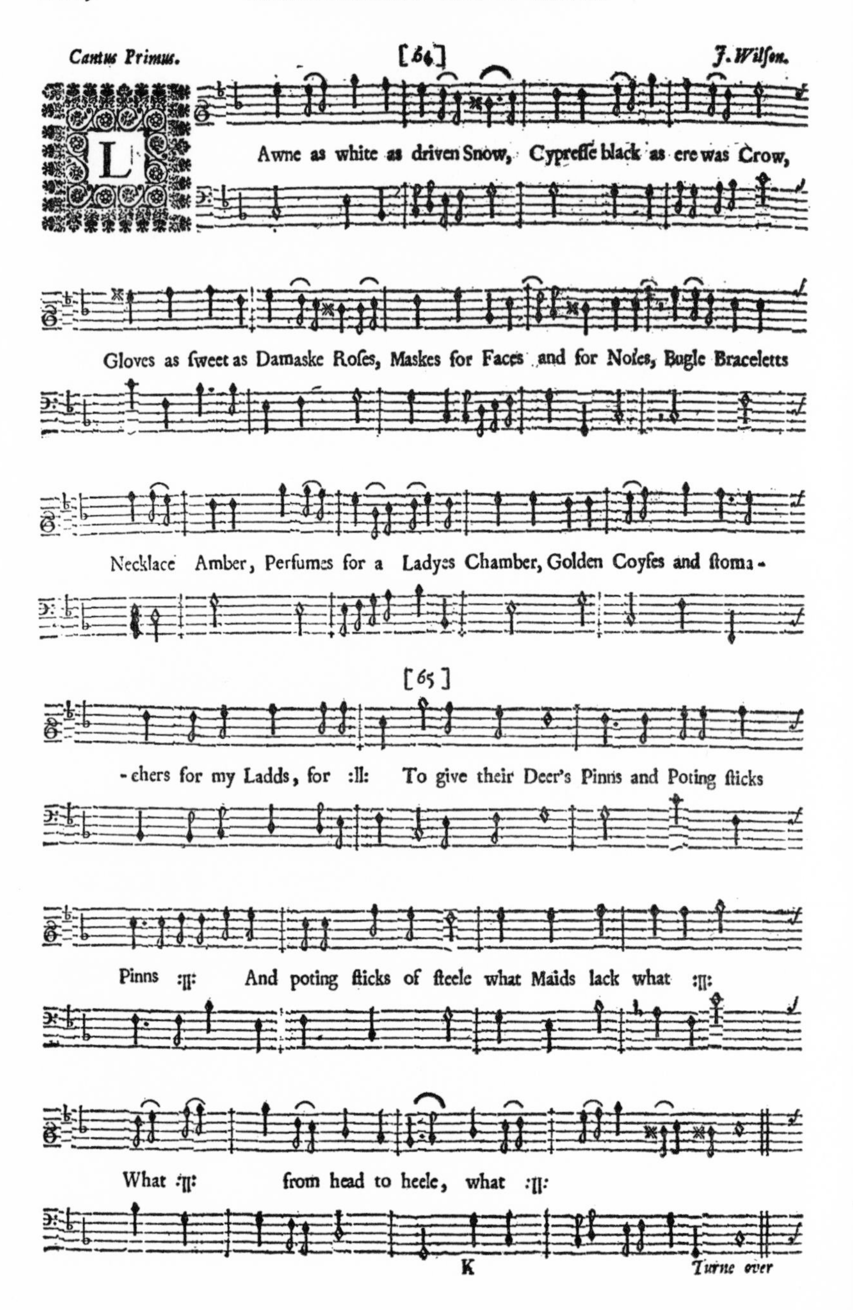
Cantus Primus.
[64]
J. Wilson.
L
Awne as white as driven Snow, Cypresse black as ere was Crow,
Gloves as sweet as Damaske Roses, Maskes for Faces and for Noses, Bugle Braceletts
Necklace Amber, Perfumes for a Ladyes Chamber, Golden Coyfes and stoma-
[65]
-chers for my Ladds, for :ll: To give their Deer's Pinns and Poting sticks
Pinns :||: And poting sticks of steele what Maids lack what :||:
What :||: from head to heele, what :||:
K
Turne over

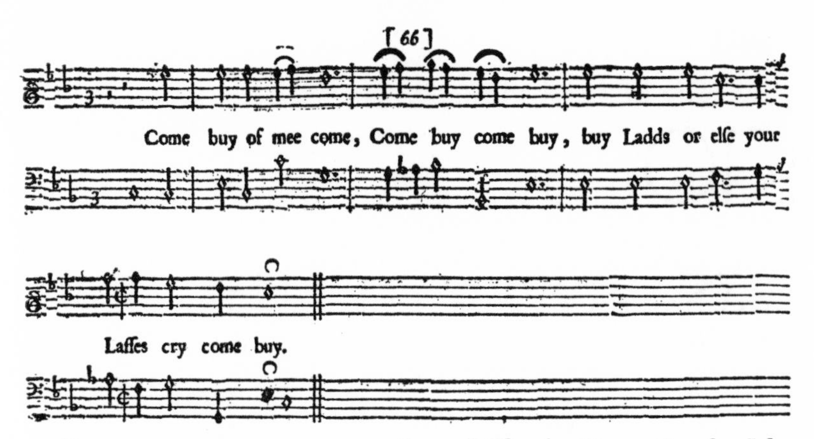
[66]
Come buy of mee come, Come buy come buy, buy Ladds or elſe your
Laſſes cry come buy.

"LAWNE AS WHITE AS DRIVEN SNOW." The familiar setting by John Wilson. *Source:* John Wilson, *Cheerfull Ayres* (1660).

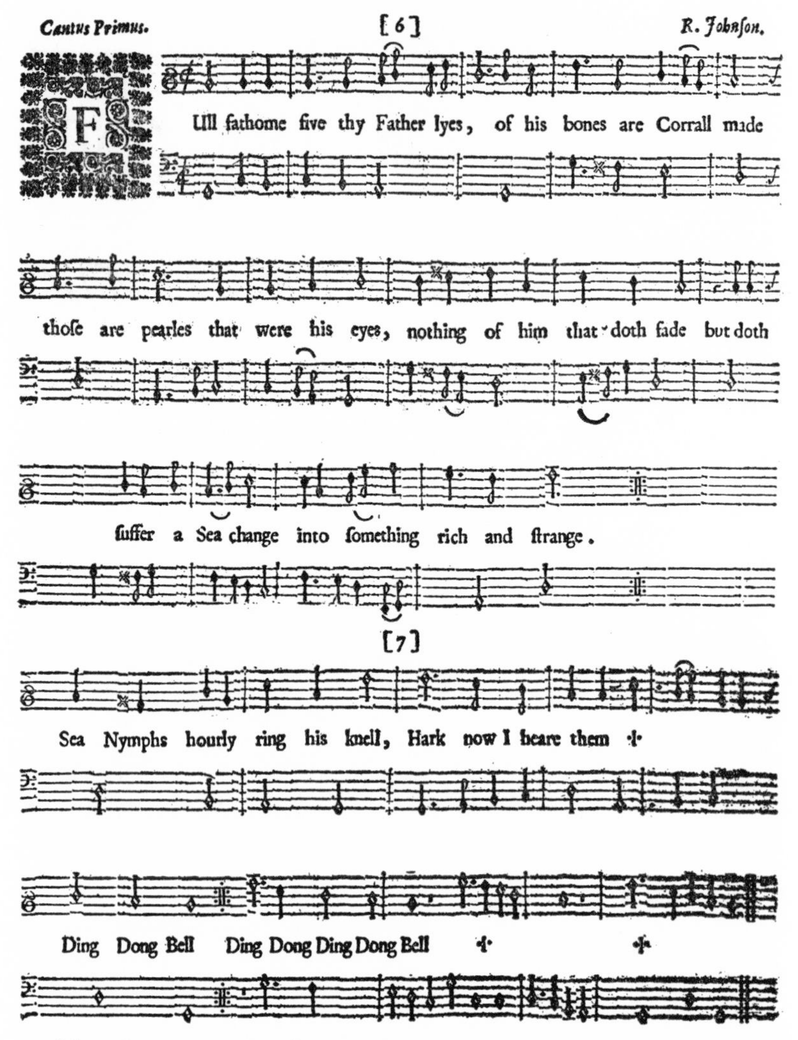
Cantus Primus.
[6]
R. Johnson.
F
Ull fathome five thy Father lyes, of his bones are Corrall made
those are pearles that were his eyes, nothing of him that doth fade but doth
suffer a Sea change into something rich and strange.
[7]
Sea Nymphs hourly ring his knell, Hark now I heare them
Ding Dong Bell Ding Dong Ding Dong Bell

"FULL FATHOME FIVE." Set by Robert Johnson, probably for the revival of *The Tempest* in 1613. *Source:* John Wilson, *Cheerfull Ayres* (1660).

FACING

"THE TEMPEST" and "A MASQUE." Professor John Cutts believes that both pieces of music were performed in the 1613 revival of *The Tempest*. *Source:* British Museum Add. MS 10444.

62
The Tempest
63
A Masque.
62
The Tempest
63
A Masque.

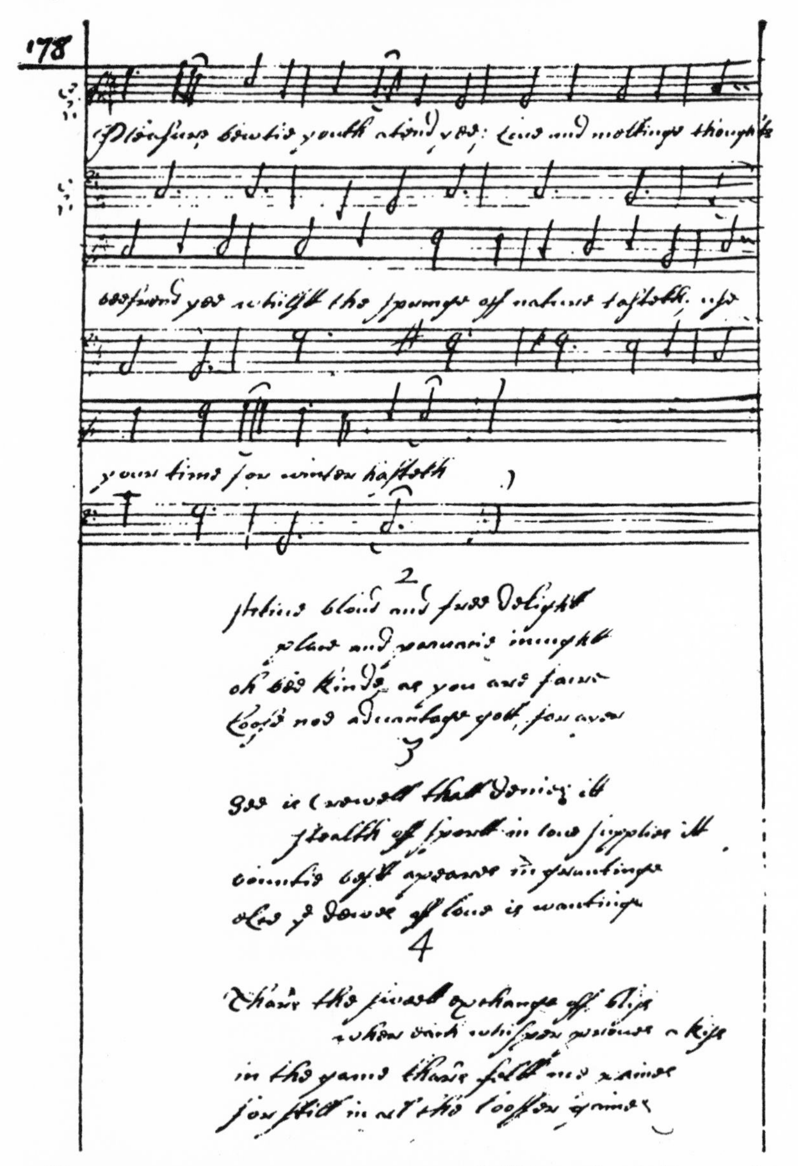

"PLEASURE, BEWTIE, YOUTH ATEND YOU." The music of this song by William Lawes I have used as a setting for the nuptial song of Juno and Ceres in *The Tempest*. *Source:* New York Public Library MS Drexel 4257 (John Gamble's Commonplace Book of Songs, 1659).

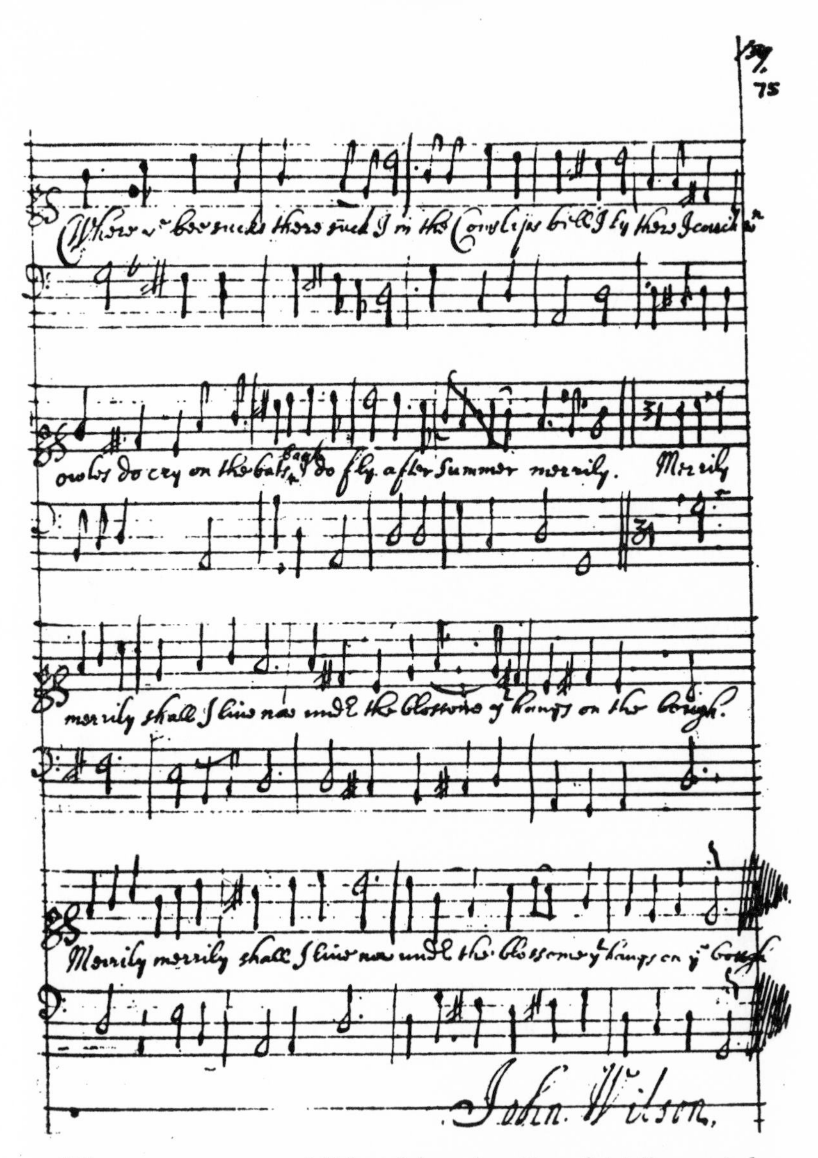

"WHERE YE BEE SUCKS." Robert Johnson's setting of Ariel's song is here ascribed, probably in error, to John Wilson. This version, to my knowledge, has not been published before. *Source:* Bodleian Library Ms Don. c. 57.

Bibliography

(Note: Most of the following entries are supplementary to those listed in the first book of this series, *Shakespeare's Use of Music: a Study of the Music and Its Performance in the Original Production of Seven Comedies.)*

ADAMS, J. *The Globe Playhouse: Its Design and Equipment.* Cambridge: Harvard University Press, 1942.

————. "The Staging of 'The Tempest,' III, iii," *RES, XIV* (October, 1938), 404-419.

ARBEAU, T. (Jehan Tabourot). *Orchesography* (1588). New York: Kamin Dance Publishers, 1948.

ARKWRIGHT, G. *The Music of Campion's Masque for Lord Hayes* (1607). London: Joseph Williams, 1889.

BACON, F. *The Works of Francis Bacon, Lord Chancellor of England,* edited by Basil Montagu. Philadelphia: A. Hart, Late Carey & Hart, 1853. 3 vols.

BANKE, C. DE. *Shakespearean Stage Production: Then & Now.* New York: McGraw-Hill Book Co., Inc., 1953.

BANTOCK, G. *One Hundred Songs of England.* Boston: Oliver Ditson Co., 1914.

BARNES, J. *The Praise of Musicke: wherein besides the antiquitie, dignitie, delectation, & use there-of in civil matters, is also declared the sober and lawfull use of the same in the congregation and Church of God. . . . Printed at Oxenford by Ioseph Barnes Printer to the Universitie, Anno 1586.* Huntington Library (STC 20184).

BEAUMONT, F. "The Masque of the Inner Temple and Gray's Inn, Gray's Inn and the Inner Temple," in Anon., *Who Wrote the Masque of "The Marriage of the Thames and Rhine?"* n.d.

BECK, S. "The Case of 'O Mistresse Mine,'" *Renaissance News,* VI (Summer, 1953), 19-23.

BEDBROOK, G. *Keyboard Music from the Middle Ages to the Beginnings of the Baroque.* London, New York: Macmillan Co., 1949.

BOWDEN, W. *The English Dramatic Lyric, 1603-42: A Study in Stuart Dramatic Technique.* New Haven: Yale University Press, 1951.

BRONSON, B. "Daisies Pied and Icicles," *MLN,* LXIII (January, 1948), 35-38.

BUKOFZER, M. *Music in the Baroque Era from Monteverdi to Bach.* New York: W. W. Norton & Co., Inc., 1947.

BURTON, R. *The Anatomy of Melancholy, What it is. With all the kindes, causes, symptomes, prog-nostickes, and severall cures of it. In three maine partitions with their severall Sections, Members, and Subsec-tions. Philosophically, Medicinally, Historically, Ope-ned and cut up. By Democritus Iunior. With a Satyricall Preface, conducing to the following Discourse. Macrob. Omne meum, Nihil meum. At Oxford, Printed by Iohn Lichfield and Iames Short, for Henry Cripps, Anno-Dom. 1621.* Folger Shakespeare Library.

CAMPBELL, L. *Scenes and Machines on the English Stage during the Renaissance.* Cambridge: Harvard University Press, 1923.

CAMPION, T. *Campion's Works,* edited by P. Vivian. Oxford: The Clarendon Press, 1909.

————. *The Description of a Maske: Presented in the Banqueting roome at Whitehall, on Saint Stephens night last, At the Mariage of the Right Honourable the Earle of Somerset: And the right noble the Lady Frances Howard. Written by Thomas Campion. Where unto are annexed divers choyse Ayres composed for this Maske that may be sung with a single voyce to the Lute or Base-Viall. London Printed by E. A. for Lawrence Lisle, dwelling in Paules Church yard, at the signe of the Tygers head. 1614.* Folger Shakespeare Library.

CARPENTER, N. "Music in 'Doctor Faustus': Two Notes," *N&Q,* CXCV (April, 1950), 180, 181.

————. "Musicians in Early University Drama," *N&Q,* CXCV (October, 1950), 470-472.

CHAMBERS, SIR E. *The Elizabethan Stage.* Oxford: The Clarendon Press, 1923 (reprinted 1945). 4 vols.

————. *William Shakespeare: A Study of Facts and Problems.* Oxford: The Clarendon Press, 1930. 2 vols.

CHAMBERS, R. "The Jacobean Shakespeare and Measure for Measure," *Proceedings of the British Academy,* XXIII. London: Humphrey Milford, 1937.

CHAPMAN, G. *The Memorable Masque of the Two Honourable Houses or Innes of Court; the Middle Temple, and Lincolnes Inne. As It was Performed Before the King, at White-hall on Shrove Munday at night; being the 15. of Febr. 1613. At the Princely Celebration of the most royall Nuptials of the Palsgrave, and his thrice gratious Princesse Elizabeth, &c. With a description of their whole show, in the manner of their march on horse backe to the Court, from the Master of the Rolls his house: with all their right Noble consorts, and most showfull attendants. Invented, and fashioned, with the ground, and speciall structure of the whole worke: By our Kingdomes most Artfull and Ingenious Architect Inigo Iones. Supplied, Applied, Digested, and written, By Geo. Chapman. At London, Printed by F. K. for George Norton, and are to be sold at his shop neere Temple-barre.* Folger Shakespeare Library.

————. *The Plays and Poems of George Chapman,* edited by T. M. Parrott. London: George Routledge & Sons, Ltd., 1914. 2 vols.

CHAPPELL, W. *Popular Music of the Olden Time; A Collection of Ancient Songs, Ballads, and Dance Tunes, Illustrative of the National Music of England. With a Short Introduction to the Different Reigns, and Notices of the Airs from Writers of the Sixteenth and Seventeenth Centuries. Also a Short Account of the Minstrels. By W. Chappell, F.S.A. The Whole of the Airs Harmonized by G. A. MacFarren.* London: Cramer, Beale, & Chappell, n.d. 2 vols.

————. *Old English Popular Music,* edited by H. E. Wooldridge. New York: Novello, Ewer & Co., 1893. 2 vols.

CURRY, W. *Shakespeare's Philosophical Patterns.* Baton Rouge: Louisiana State University Press, 1937.

CUTTS, J. "An Unpublished Contemporary Setting of a Shakespeare Song," *Shakespeare Survey 9,* 1956, pp. 86-89.

CUTTS, J. "Jacobean Masque and Stage Music," *Music & Letters,* XXXV (July, 1954), 185-200.

————. "Music and the Supernatural in 'The Tempest': a Study in Interpretation," *Music & Letters,* XXXIX (October, 1958), 347-358.

————. "The Original Music to Middleton's 'The Witch,'" *SQ,* VII (Spring, 1956), 203-209.

————. "Robert Johnson: King's Musician in His Majesty's Public Entertainment," *Music & Letters,* XXXVI (April, 1955), 110-125.

————. "Two Jacobean Theatre Songs," *Music & Letters,* XXXIII (October, 1952), 333, 334.

DANKS, H. "The Viola d'Amore," *Music & Letters,* XXXVIII (January, 1957), 14-20.

DART, T. "Lord Herbert of Cherbury's Lute-book," *Music & Letters,* XXXVIII (April, 1957), 136-148.

————. "Morley's 'Consort Lessons' of 1599," *Proceedings of the Royal Musical Association,* November, 1947.

————. "The Printed Fantasies of Orlando Gibbons," *Music & Letters,* XXXVII (October, 1956), 342-349.

DAVIES, SIR J. *Orchestra or A Poem of Dancing,* edited by E. M. W. Tillyard. London: Chatto & Windus, 1947.

DELAUZE, F. *Apologie de la Danse (1623): A treatise of instruction in dancing and deportment,* edited and translated by J. Wildeblood. London: Frederick Muller Ltd., 1952.

DENT, E. "Shakespeare and Music," *A Companion to Shakespeare Studies,* edited by Harley Granville-Barker and G. B. Harrison. Cambridge: The University Press, 1934.

DOLMETSCH, M. *Dances of England and France from 1450 to 1600: With Their Music and Authentic Manner of Performance.* London: Routledge and Kegan Paul, Ltd., 1949.

DUCKLES, V. "The 'Curious Art' of John Wilson (1595-1674): An Introduction to His Songs and Lute Music," *JAMS,* VII (Summer, 1954), 93-112.

————. "The Gamble Manuscript as a Source of 'Continuo' Song in England," *JAMS,* I (Summer, 1948), 23-40.

————. "Jacobean Theatre Songs," *Music & Letters,* XXXIV (January, 1953), 88, 89.

————. "New Light on 'O Mistresse Mine,'" *Renaissance News,* VII (Autumn, 1954), 98-100.

Elizabethan Song Book, An: Lute Songs, Madrigals, and Rounds, edited by N. Greenberg, W. H. Auden and C. Kallman. Garden City, N. Y.: Doubleday & Co., Inc., 1955.

ELYOT, SIR T. *The Gouernour.* New York: E. P. Dutton & Co., 1937.

EVANS, H. *English Masques.* London: Gresham Publishing Co., 1897.

EVANS, W. *Henry Lawes; Musician and Friend of Poets.* New York: Modern Language Association of America, 1941.

————. "Shakespeare's 'Harke, Harke, ye Larke,'" *PMLA,* LX (1945), 98-103.

FELLOWES, E. *The English School of Lutenist Song Writers.* New York: G. Schirmer Co., 1920-1932 (1st Series, 16 vols.). London: Stainer & Bell Ltd., 1925-1927 (2nd Series, 8 vols.).

Fitzwilliam Virginal Book: Selected Pieces. Leipzig: Breitkopf & Härtel, n.d. 2 vols.

GIBBON, J. *Melody and the Lyric from Chaucer to the Cavaliers.* New York: E. P. Dutton & Co., Inc., 1930.

GOMBOSI, O. "Some Musical Aspects of the English Court Masque," *JAMS,* I (Fall, 1948), 3-19.

GOWER, J. *The Complete Works of John Gower,* edited by G. C. Macaulay. Oxford: The Clarendon Press, 1901.

HODGES, C. *The Globe Restored: A Study of the Elizabethan Theatre.* London: Ernest Benn Ltd., 1953.

HOLBORNE, A. *Pavans, galliards, almains, and other short aeirs both graue, and light, in fiue parts, for viols, violins, or other musicall wind instruments. Made by Anthony Holborne . . . London, imprinted by William Barley, the assignee of Thomas Morley, 1599.* Huntington Library (STC 13563).

HORSLEY, I. "The Renaissance Attitude Toward Interpretation in Instrumental Performance," *Renaissance News,* X (Summer, 1957), 79-85.

HOTSON, L. *The First Night of "Twelfth Night."* New York: Macmillan Co., 1954.

————. "Shakespeare's Arena," *The Sewanee Review,* LXI (Summer, 1953), 347-361.

HUME, T. *Captaine Humes Poeticall Musicke. Principally made for two Basse-Viols, yet so contrived, that it may be plaied 8. severall waies upon sundry Instruments with much facilitie . . . Composed by Tobias Hume Gentleman. London Printed by John Windet. 1607.* Folger Shakespeare Library.

ING, C. *Elizabethan Lyrics: A Study in the Development of English Metres and their Relation to Poetic Effect.* London: Chatto & Windus, 1951.

INGRAM, R. "The Use of Music in the Plays of Marston," *Music & Letters,* XXXVII (April, 1956), 154-164.

ISAACS, J. "Production and Stage Management at the Blackfriars Theatre," *Shakespeare Association Pamphlet,* 1933.

IZON, J. "Italian Musicians at the Tudor Court," *Musical Quarterly,* XLIV (July, 1958), 329-337.

JONSON, B. *Ben Jonson,* edited by C. H. Herford, P. and E. Simpson. Oxford: The Clarendon Press, 1925-1952. 11 vols.

KERNODLE, G. *From Art to Theatre: Form and Convention in the Renaissance.* Chicago: University of Chicago Press, 1947.

KIDSON, F. "A Study of Old English Song and Popular Melody Prior to the 19th Century," *Musical Quarterly,* I (October, 1915), 569-582.

KNIGHT, G. *The Crown of Life.* London: Methuen & Co., Ltd., 1948.

————. *The Shakespearian Tempest: With a Chart of Shakespeare's Dramatic Universe.* London: Methuen & Co., Ltd., 1953.

LAW, E. "Shakespeare's Tempest as originally produced at Court," *Shakespeare Association Bulletin,* 1920.

LAWRENCE, W. "The Masque in the Tempest," *Fortnightly Review,* XIII (1920), 941-946.

————. *Pre-Restoration Stage Studies.* Cambridge: Harvard University Press, 1927.

————. *Shakespeare's Workshop.* Boston: Houghton Mifflin Co., 1928.

LAWRENCE, W. "Thomas Ravenscroft's Theatrical Association," *MLR*, XIX (October, 1924), 418-423.

LEWIS, A. *William Shakespeare. Two Songs from the Tempest set by his contemporary Robert Johnson with two other songs by the same composer.* Paris: Lyrebird Press, 1936.

LONG, J. "Another Masque for 'The Merry Wives of Windsor,'" *SQ*, III (January, 1952), 39-43.

————. "Laying the Ghosts in 'Pericles,'" *SQ*, VII (Winter, 1956), 39-42

————. *Shakespeare's Use of Music: A Study of the Music and Its Performance in the Original Production of Seven Comedies.* Gainesville: The University of Florida Press, 1955.

MACKERNESS, E. "Morley's Musical Sensibility," *Cambridge Journal*, II, 301-308.

MANIFOLD, J. *The Music in English Drama from Shakespeare to Purcell.* London: Rockliff Publishing Corp., 1956.

————. "Theatre Music in the Sixteenth and Seventeenth Centuries," *Music & Letters*, XXIX (October, 1948), 390-391.

MARSTON, J. *The Works of John Marston,* edited by A. H. Bullen. London: John C. Nimmo, 1887. 3 vols.

McCULLEN, J. "The Functions of Songs Aroused by Madness in Elizabethan Drama," *A Tribute to George Coffin Taylor: Studies and Essays.* Chapel Hill: University of North Carolina Press, 1952.

McMANAWAY, J. "Songs and Masques in 'The Tempest,'" *Theatre Miscellany: Six Pieces Connected with the Seventeenth-century Stage.* Luttrell Society, No. 14, pp. 69-96.

MERSENNE, M. *Traité de L'Harmonie Universelle. Oú est contenu la Musique Theorique & Pratique des Anciens & Modernes, avec les causes de ses effets. Enrichie de Raisons prises de la Philosophie, & Mathematiques. Par le sieur de Sermes. A Paris, Pour Guillaume Baudry, ruë des Amandiers, prés le College des Graffins, M.D.C. XXVII. Avec Privilege du Roy.* Folger Shakespeare Library (STC 1820).

MEYER, E. *Die mehrstimmige Spielmusik des 17. Yahrhunderts in Nord und Mitteleuropa.* Kassel, 1934.

————. *English Chamber Music: The History of a Great Art from the Middle Ages to Purcell.* London: Lawrence Wishart, 1946.

————. "The 'In Nomine' and the Birth of Polyphonic Instrumental Style in England," *Music & Letters*, XVII (January, 1936), 25-36.

MILLER, H. "English Plainsong Combinations for Keyboard in the Sixteenth Century," *Harvard University Summaries of Theses*, 1943-1945.

MOORE, J. "The Function of the Songs in Shakespeare's Plays," *Shakespeare Studies by Members of the Department of English of the University of Wisconsin.* Madison, 1916, 78-102.

————. "The Songs of the Public Theaters in the Time of Shakespeare," *JEGP*, XXVIII (April, 1929), 166-202.

MORLEY, T. *A Plain and Easy Introduction to Practical Music,* edited by R. Harman. New York: W. W. Norton & Co., Inc., 1952.

————. *The First Booke of Consort Lessons, made by divers exquisite Authors, for six Instruments to play together, the Treble Lute, the Pandora, the Cittern, the Base-Violl, the Flute & Treble-Violl. Newly set forth at the coast & charges of a Gentleman, for his private pleasure, and for divers others his frendes which delight in Musicke. Printed at London in Little Saint Helens by William Barley, the Assigne of Thomas Morley, and are to be solde at his shop in Gratious-streete. Cum privilegio ad Imprimendum solum. 1599.* (Cittern, treble viol parts only.) New York Public Library copy.

————. *The First Booke of Consort Lessons, made by divers exquisite Authors, for sixe Instruments to play together: viz. the Treble Lute, the Pandora, the Citterne, the Base-Violl, the Flute, and the Treble-Violl. Collected by Thomas Morley, Gentleman, and now newly corrected and inlarged. LONDON: Printed by Thomas Snodham for Iohn Browne, and are to be sould at his shop in S. Duustones Church-yard in Fleet-street. The Assigne of William Barley. 1611.* (Flute, Pandora parts only.) Huntington Library copy.

Musique Instrumentale de la Renaissance, La, edited by J. Jacquot. Paris: Editions du Centre National de la Recherche Scientifique, 1955.

Musique et Poésie au XVIe siècle. Paris: Editions du Centre National de la Recherche Scientifique, 1954.

NAGLER, A. *Sources of Theatrical History.* New York: Theatre Annual, Inc., 1952.

NAYLOR, E. *Shakespeare and Music, With Illustrations from the Music of the 16th and 17th Centuries.* New York: E. P. Dutton and Co., Inc., 1931.

NICOLL, A. *Stuart Masques and the Renaissance Stage.* London: George G. Harrap & Co., Ltd., 1937.

NOBLE, R. "Shakespeare's Songs and Stage," *A Series of Papers on Shakespeare and the Theatre.* Shakespeare Association. London: Humphrey Milford, 1927.

————. *Shakespeare's Use of Song, with the Text of the Principal Songs.* London: Humphrey Milford, 1923.

NOSWORTHY, J. M. "Music and Its Function in the Romances of Shakespeare," *Shakespeare Survey 11,* Cambridge: Cambridge University Press, 1958, pp. 60-69.

Oxford Companion to Music, The, edited by P. Scholes. London: Oxford University Press, 1947.

PEELE, G. "The Arraignment of Paris," in *English Drama 1580-1642,* edited by C. F. T. Brooke and N. B. Paradise. New York: D. C. Heath and Co., 1933.

PLAYFORD, J. *Catch that Catch can; or the musical Companion . . . Dialogues, Glees, Ayres, and Ballads, of two, three, and four Voyces . . . London,* 1673. Huntington Library.

————. *Select musical Ayres and Dialogues, in 3 Divisions: first, Ayres for a Voyce alone, to the Theorbo, or Base-Viol; second, Choice Dialogues for 2 Voyces, for 2 ditto; third, Short Ayres and Songs of 3 Voyces, which may be sung by one or two Voices to an Instrument. London. 1653.* Huntington Library.

RATSEY, G. *The Life and Death of Gamaliel Ratsey a famous thief, of England, Executed at Bedford the 26th of March last past. 1605.* Published for the Shakespeare Association by Humphrey Milford, Oxford University Press, 1935.

RAVENSCROFT, T. *A Briefe Discourse of the true (but neglected) use of Charact'ring the Degrees, by their Perfection, Imperfection and Diminu-*

tion in Measurable Musicke, against the Common Practise and Custome of these Times. Examples whereof are exprest in the Harmony of 4 Voyces, concerning the Pleasure of 5 usuall Recreations. 1. Hunting. 2. Hawking. 3. Dancing 4. Drinking. 5. Enamouring (1614). Huntington Library.

REED, E. *Songs from the British Drama.* New Haven: Yale University Press, 1925.

REESE, G. *Music in the Renaissance.* New York: W. W. Norton & Co., Inc., 1954.

————. "The Origin of the English 'In Nomine,'" *JAMS,* II (Spring, 1949), 7-22.

ROWEN, R. *Early Chamber Music.* New York: Columbia University Press, 1949.

SCHOLES, P. "The Purpose behind Shakespeare's Use of Music," *Proceedings of the Royal Music Association.* 1917.

SENG, P. *The Dramatic Function of the Songs in Shakespeare's Plays.* Unpublished dissertation, Harvard University, 1955.

SHAKESPEARE, W. *The Works of Shakespeare,* edited by E. Malone. London, 1790. 10 vols.

————. *The Complete Plays and Poems of William Shakespeare,* edited by W. A. Neilson and C. J. Hill. New York: Houghton Mifflin Co., 1942.

————. *The Complete Works of Shakespeare,* edited by H. Craig. New York: Scott, Foresman and Co., 1951.

————. *Shakespeare: Twenty-three Plays and the Sonnets,* edited by T. M. Parrott. New York: Charles Scribner's Sons, 1938.

————. *Mr. William Shakespeares Comedies, Histories, & Tragedies: Published according to the True Originall Copies. London Printed by Isaac Iaggard, and E. Blount.* 1623. Reduced facsimile. New York: Funk & Wagnalls, Publishers, 1887.

————. *Mr. William Shakespeares Comedies, Histories & Tragedies: A facsimile edition prepared by Helge Kökeritz with an Introduction by Charles Tyler Prouty.* New Haven: Yale University Press, 1954.

————. *All's Well That Ends Well,* edited by W. O. Brigstocke, Arden edition. London: Methuen and Co., 1904. Vol. 1.

————. *All's Well that Ends Well,* edited by D. Wilson and A. Quiller-Couch. Cambridge: The University Press, 1955.

————. *Cymbeline,* edited by H. H. Furness, Variorum edition. Philadelphia: J. P. Lippincott & Co., 1913. Vol. 18.

————. *Measure for Measure,* edited by H. C. Hart, Arden edition. London: Methuen and Co., 1905. Vol. 22.

————. *Measure for Measure,* edited by D. Wilson and A. Quiller-Couch. Cambridge: The University Press, 1922.

————. *A most pleasant and excellent conceited Comedie, of Syr Iohn Falstaffe, and the merrie Wives of Windsor Entermixed with sundrie variable and pleasing humors of Syr Hugh the Welch Knight, Iustice Shallow, and his wise Cousin M. Slender. With the swaggering vaine of Auncient Pistoll, and Corporall Nym. By William Shakespeare. As it hath bene divers times Acted by the right Honorable my Lord Chamberlaines servants. Both before her Maiestie, and elsewhere. London Printed by T. C. for Arthur Iohnson, and are to be sold at his shop in Powles*

Church-yard, at the signe of the Flower de Leuse and the Crowne. 1602. Folger Shakespeare Library Quarto.

————. *The Merry Wives of Windsor,* edited by H. C. Hart, Arden edition. London: Methuen and Co., 1904. Vol. 24.

————. *Pericles,* edited by K. Deighton, Arden edition. London: Methuen and Co., 1925. Vol. 28.

————. *Pericles,* edited by J. C. Maxwell. Cambridge: Cambridge University Press, 1956.

————. *The Late, And much admired Play, Called Pericles, Prince of Tyre. With the true Relation of the whole Historie, adventures, and fortunes of the said Prince: As also, The no lesse strange, and worthy accidents, in the Birth and Life, of his Daughter Mariana. As it hath been divers and sundry times acted by his Maiesties servants, at the Globe on the Banck-side. By William Shakespeare. Imprinted at London for Henry Gosson, and are to be sold at the signe of the Sunne in Pater-noster row, &c. 1609.* Folger Shakespeare Library Quarto 1609(1).

————. *The Tempest,* edited by G. L. Kittredge. Boston: Ginn & Co., 1939.

————. *The Tempest,* edited by M. Luce, Arden edition. London: Methuen and Co., 1909-1924. Vol. 31.

————. *The Tempest,* edited by F. Kermode, Arden edition. London: Methuen and Co., 1954.

————. *The Tempest,* edited by H. H. Furness, Variorum edition. J. P. Lippincott & Co., 1918. Vol. 9.

————. *The Winter's Tale,* edited by H. H. Furness, Variorum edition. Philadelphia: J. P. Lippincott & Co., 1926. Vol. 11.

SISSON, C. J. "The Magic of Prospero," *Shakespeare Survey 11.* Cambridge: Cambridge University Press, 1958, pp. 70-77.

Songs and Lyrics from the English Playbooks, edited by F. Boas. London: Cresset Press, 1945.

SPITZER, L. "Classical and Christian Ideas of World Harmony: Prolegomena to an Interpretation of the Word 'Stimmung,'" *Traditio,* II (1944), 409-464, and III (1945), 307-364.

STERNFELD, F. "The Dramatic and Allegorical Function of Music in Shakespeare's Tragedies," *Annales Musicologique,* III, Paris, 1955.

————. "*Troilus and Cressida:* Music for the Play," *English Institute Essays 1952,* edited by A. Downer. New York: Columbia University Press, 1954, pp. 107-137.

STRUNK, O. *Source Readings in Music History from Classical Antiquity through the Romantic Era.* New York: W. W. Norton & Co., 1950.

SUBIRA, J. *Historia de la Música Teatral en España.* Barcelona: Editorial Labor, S.A., 1945.

THEWLIS, G. "Some Notes on a Bodleian Manuscript," *Music & Letters,* XXII (January, 1941), 32-35.

THORNDIKE, A. *The Influence of Beaumont and Fletcher on Shakespeare.* Worcester, Mass.: Press of O. B. Wood, 1901.

TITCOMB, C. "Baroque Court and Military Trumpets and Kettledrums, Technique and Music," *The Galpin Society Journal,* IX (June, 1956), 56-81.

TURBERVILLE, G. *The Noble Arte of Venerie or Hunting. Wherein is handled and set out the Vertues, Nature, and Properties of fivetene sun-*

drie Chaces togither, with the order and maner how to Hunte and kill every one of them. Translated and collected for the pleasure of all Noblemen and Gentlemen, out of the best approved Authors, which have written anything concerning the same: And reduced into such order and proper termes as are used here, in this noble Realme of England. (1575.) Folger Shakespeare Library (STC 24328).

TWYNE, L. *The patterne of Painfull Adventures.* New Rochelle, N. Y.: Elston Press, 1903.

UHLER, J. *Morley's Canzonets for Two Voices.* Baton Rouge: Louisiana State University Press, 1954.

ULRICH, H. *Chamber Music: The Growth and Practice of an Intimate Art.* New York: Columbia University Press, 1948.

VLASTO, J. "An Elizabethan Anthology of Rounds," *Musical Quarterly,* (April, 1954), 222-234.

WALKER, E. *A History of Music in England.* New York: Oxford University Press, 1952.

WARD, J. "The 'Dolfull Domps.'" *JAMS,* IV (Summer, 1951), 111-121.

WHETSTONE, G. *THE RIGHT EXCELlent and famous Historye, of* Promos *and* Cassandra: *Devided into two Commicall Discourses. In the fyrste parte is showne, the unsufferable abuse, of a lewde Magistrate: The vertuous behaviours of a chaste Ladye: The uncontrowled leawdenes of a favoured Curtisan. And the undeserved estimation of a pernicious parasyte. In the second parte is discoursed, the perfect magnanimitye of a noble Kinge, in checking Vice and favouringe Vertue: Wherein is showne, the Ruyne and over-throwe, of dishonest practises: with the advancement of upright dealing. The worke of George Whetstones Gent.* Formae nulla fides. Folger Shakespeare Library.

WILSON, J. *Cheerfull Ayres or Ballads First composed for one single Voice and since set for three Voices by John Wilson Dr in Musick Professor of the same in the University of Oxford. Oxford. Printed by W. Hall, for Ric Davis. Anno Dom. MDCLX.* Folger Shakespeare Library.

WOODFILL, W. *Musicians in English Society from Elizabeth to Charles I.* Princeton, N. J.: Princeton University Press, 1953.

Index